WINTHROP N. KELLOGG

and Sonar

THE UNIVERSITY OF CHICAGO PRESS

The University of Chicago Press, Chicago 37
The University of Toronto Press, Toronto 5, Canada
© 1961 by The University of Chicago.   Published 1961
Composed and printed in the U.S.A.

61-11294
6-24-61

2

Porpoises and Sonar

Porpoises

I have met with a story, which, although authenticated by undoubted evidence, looks very like a fable.

—PLINY THE YOUNGER
(*Letters* ix. 33)

Preface

The object or purpose of this book is to describe a kind of scientific adventure. It is an adventure of excitement and discovery, involving one of the most unusual and intelligent of all animals—the bottlenose dolphin or porpoise. The adventure began in 1951, when it dawned upon us for the first time that anyone who had not become personally acquainted with this fascinating animal was missing something really fine. Our first published reference to the possibility of porpoise sonar appeared shortly afterward in a report in the journal *Science* (Kellogg and Kohler, 1952). This beginning led to the development of an extensive research program which has been going on, in one form or another, until the present time.

The surroundings and requirements of the research turned out to be quite different from those which obtain in traditional studies of animal behavior. Instead of being confined in an experimental room with laboratory rats, dogs, or monkeys, we often found ourselves running around in swimming trunks on some sandy beach. Instead of building research apparatus with properties like hardware cloth, tin shears, and soldering irons, we were operating on a grand scale with such things as telephone poles, half-inch steel cable, and acetylene torches. Nearly all the equipment was used under water, and some of it had to be constructed there. Hence, we became skin and helmet divers. We also made observations from skiffs, from motorboats, and from sailboats. Needless to say, it was all a great deal of fun.

The program as a whole examines the way in which porpoises navigate in the ocean without the use of vision, smell, taste, or touch. It attempts to answer the question of how they "see with their ears." It presents evidence showing the workings of their echo-ranging or sonar system. It explains how they avoid obstacles while swimming at night or in turbid water, and how they locate fish for food.

In order to obtain data on such questions, it has been necessary to investigate a number of specific problems—all within the general scope of the over-all plan. We have, therefore, studied the sounds which porpoises emit in water and have made an acoustical analysis of these noises as echo-ranging signals. We have tested the hearing of living animals and have dissected the ears and examined the brain cavity of some which were dead. We have observed their reactions to different kinds of water-borne noises and to different sorts of sound-reflecting targets. We have watched captive porpoises as they swam through an obstacle course or avoided invisible surfaces of glass or clear plastic. And we obtained some evidence of their ability to distinguish between targets of varying size and density by auditory perception alone.

Since the detection of submerged objects is of great importance to marine navigation, the remarkable properties of the dolphin's sonar system are of interest to the United States Navy. What these animals can do has a definite bearing on our national defense, as a means of improving man-made sonar. To help our investigations along these lines we visited the U.S. Navy Electronics Laboratory at Point Loma, California, the Underwater

Sound Reference Laboratory at Orlando, Florida, and the Mine Defense Center at Panama City, Florida. We have also made trips to research centers in Washington, D.C., to the Lerner Marine Laboratory at Bimini in the Bahama Islands (a field station of the American Museum of Natural History), to Key West, to Marineland, Florida, and to numerous other stations within the state of Florida. A special voyage from Mobile, Alabama, across the Gulf of Mexico, to the Yucatan Peninsula was taken on the Coast Guard cutter "Tampa." Some of these research trips led to positive results; others were less fruitful or entirely negative.

The project as a whole was sponsored and supported by the Office of Naval Research and the National Science Foundation. The ONR lent indispensable underwater sound gear, and the NSF gave financial aid in the form of substantial research grants. Additional funds for carrying on the work were obtained from the Psychology Department, the Oceanographic Institute, and the Research Council of Florida State University. All the research which was conducted was unclassified from a military standpoint.

No program of this nature can be accomplished without the help and co-operation of many persons. We should therefore like to acknowledge the generous aid and assistance of numerous graduate students who worked on various aspects of the project, and of professors in other disciplines who contributed willingly of their specialized knowledge. The encouragement of Dr. Harold J. Humm, now of Duke University, was so important during the early stages that the research might never have begun without him. We were also helped by Dr. Samuel L. Meyer, of the College of the Pacific, and by Dr. Franklin C. W. Olson, of the RCA Laboratories at Princeton, New Jersey.

Dr. Arvord W. Belden, Dr. Bruce P. Carpenter, Dr. Richard F. Patteson, Mr. James L. Dowis, and Mr. Richard W. Shoenberger acted at different times as research assistants. Of invaluable and continuous aid was the fine co-operation of Mr.

Robert Kohler, electronics engineer, and Mr. Richard Durant, superintendent of the Marine Laboratories of Florida State University.

Indispensable assistance in sound-recording and acoustics was furnished by Mr. Harold M. Morris of the Air Force Missile Test Center at Cape Canaveral, Florida. It was only by permission of Dr. C. M. Breder, Jr., of the American Museum of Natural History in New York City, that we were able to work at the Lerner Laboratory. We also wish to thank Mr. K. L. Sherman of the U.S. Navy Mine Defense Center at Panama City, Florida, who allowed us to use their Fairchild Sound Measuring and Analyzing System.

Finally, we are indebted to Mr. F. G. Wood, Jr., curator of the Marineland Research Laboratories at Marineland, Florida, who helped both in the conduct of the research and in the preparation of the book. A number of its photographic illustrations are published with his permission. And it was through his kindness that we were able to obtain two of the captive porpoises on which many of the observations were made.

The editors of *Science,* of the *American Psychological Association,* of the *Journal of Comparative and Physiological Psychology,* of the *Journal of the Acoustical Society of America,* of the *Psychological Record,* and of the *Journal of Psychology* have given their permission to reproduce a part of the material contained in several of the later chapters, which originally appeared as articles in these journals.

WINTHROP N. KELLOGG

Florida State University
Tallahassee, Florida
January, 1961

Contents

Illustrations

PLATES

TABLES

Chapter 1

Whales and Porpoises

Those who have had the good fortune to come into contact with whales or porpoises usually find themselves in a state of breathless astonishment. The things that are likely to startle the observer are the enormous dimensions of the giant whales and the grace, speed of swimming, and playfulness of their smaller relatives—the porpoises and dolphins. The dinosaurs of the geologic past are sometimes erroneously thought of as the largest animals which ever lived. Some may have weighed as much as 50 tons (Romer, 1957). But the biggest dinosaur of all would be dwarfed beside the giant whales now swimming in the oceans. A blue whale, *Balaenoptera musculus,* can reach 100 feet in length and weigh as much as 119 tons (Norman and Fraser, 1949). The most tremendous—and in some ways the most fascinating—creatures the world has ever known are not extinct. They are here, at this moment, for man to study and enjoy.

The whales, dolphins, and porpoises belong to the taxonomic order of *Cetacea.* All of them are warm-blooded, air-breathing mammals. They must continually come to the surface or they would suffocate. All give birth to their young alive and suckle them with milk. All have horizontal tail flukes. In spite of the fact that they live in the ocean, the whales and the porpoises are biologically closer to man than they are to any of the fishes. Many of the present whales possess rudimentary hind legs which are buried within the musculature of the body (Beddard, 1900; Howell, 1930). Their ancestors at one time lived on land (Carson, 1951).

THE ODONTOCETI

It is the *Odontoceti,* or toothed whales, in which we are most interested, and particularly the bottlenose dolphin or shallow-water porpoise, *Tursiops truncatus*. The *Mysticeti* or baleen whales from which whalebone is obtained possess no teeth. They eat by scooping up small organisms or "krill" in their cavernous mouths and filtering out the water by means of the whalebone sieves which are attached to the jaws. The *Odontoceti,* on the other hand, have pointed teeth with which they can seize, bite, or crush their food. The largest of the *Odontoceti* is the sperm whale, *Physeter catodon,* which reaches a length of 60 feet or more and may weigh as many tons (Norman and Fraser, 1949). Since its throat is bigger than that of the *Mysticeti,* this presumably is the sort of whale which swallowed Jonah.

THE DOLPHIN-PORPOISE QUESTION

The bottlenose dolphin, of course, is not nearly so big, although it is actually also one of the whales, as are the other porpoises and dolphins. The giant whales and the porpoises compare to one another much as a great Dane compares to a small dog. Bottlenose dolphins which are very large may reach a length of 10 or 12 feet, but measurements of a number of specimens taken off the Texas coast in the Gulf of Mexico show the average length in that locality to be closer to 8 feet (Gunter,

2

1942). The weight of a 7- or 8-foot animal would run around 300 pounds (see Plate I).

A dolphin, strictly speaking, is not a porpoise; and the term "porpoise" was originally meant to apply to other odontocetes. However, common usage leans more and more toward the designation of the bottlenose dolphin as a porpoise, and it is popularly known by that name in the United States. Since it generally remains within a few miles of shore and readily enters ocean bays and brackish rivers, it is the porpoise most often seen by landlubbers. Its triangular dorsal fin is a familiar sight to swimmers and to fishermen in many parts of the world.

Unfortunately, the term "dolphin" is not restricted entirely to the cetaceans. There are two large game fish (genus *Coryphaena*), which are also called dolphins. This often leads to some confusion. Another common error, which could only be made by the uninitiated, is to mistake a swimming porpoise for a shark, yet the difference in the behavior of the two is so fundamental that no one should ever make such a mistake. In swimming, a porpoise "porpoises," that is, its fin goes up and down rhythmically as it comes up to breathe. A shark will never porpoise, and its fin—when out of the water—remains in the same horizontal plane.

BLOWING OR SPOUTING

The spouting or blowing of a whale or porpoise is caused by the exhalation of air from the lungs, and the blowhole is no more than the external nostril (see Plate II). The blowholes of all cetaceans have powerful valves which can be tightly closed during submersion. The length of time which these animals can "hold their breath" and remain under water varies, of course, from species to species. The larger whales can make phenomenal dives. A sperm whale which has been harpooned, but without the use of an explosive charge, may stay below for more than an hour (Beale, 1839, p. 44). In the case of the dolphins and porpoises the maximum time is certainly much less. Some au-

3

thorities hold that the longest dive of the bottlenose dolphin is not much over 7 minutes, although Ewer (1947, p. 63) believes it to be from 10 to 15 minutes. When quiet or inactive, these animals will usually breathe from one to four times per minute. If active, the rate may be considerably faster. At night they sleep at the surface of the water.

It has been supposed that the cetaceans take in water during submersion and that this is expelled when they come to the surface—hence the term "spouting." An interesting application of this notion has been advanced by Tomilin (1947*b*). He suggests that blowing is the final stage of a process of ventilation with cool water and that a whale regulates its body temperature in this way, much as a dog takes in cool air by panting.

Another explanation, which applies particularly to the Arctic and Antarctic latitudes, is that a whale's breath simply condenses into a fountain of vapor and that the spout contains no other water than the droplets of moisture which are in the breath itself (R. Kellogg, 1940). But what of the whales which inhabit the tropical regions? We have seen sperm whales, when the external temperature of the air was over 100° F., still blow a visible spray into the air. Under such atmospheric conditions, the difference in temperature between the exhaled breath and the air would hardly be sufficient to produce condensation. Porpoises in warm climates have also been noted, on occasion, to expel a few drops of water upward from the blowhole.

A part of the water in such instances may be drawn up by suction from the wet surface of the blowhole lip and from the skin adjacent to the blowhole. But this will not account for the entire phenomenon. It is the structure of the nasal or blowhole opening which seems to be particularly important in this connection. The blowhole passage beneath the skin contains overlapping valves, as well as diverging pockets or "nasal sacs." As the animal submerges at the end of an inspiration a small quantity of water often flows inward and downward through the external orifice. More than likely this water is trapped in

4

the nasal cavities below the outer valve by the closing of the passageway beneath it. The trapped water would subsequently be blown out by the force of the exhaled air. Some human swimmers, in fact, follow a similar practice by taking water into the mouth at the end of each breath.

Just such a flow of water into the open blowhole of a bottle-nose dolphin has been recorded in slow-motion photography by Lawrence and Schevill (1956). The entire process, including the "spouting" which occurs at the end of the cycle, would appear to be no more than an incidental feature of the act of breathing.

THE SPEED OF SWIMMING

The larger whales swim at a surprisingly slow rate. A speed of 3 to 4 knots is normal for the sperm whale (Norman and Fraser, 1949, p. 263). This explains how men rowing in a whaleboat are able to overtake and capture these tremendous creatures. When disturbed or harpooned, a sperm whale may temporarily increase its speed to 10 or 12 knots. Gilmore (1959) has published interesting data on the speed and distance of swimming of a California gray whale whose estimated length was 36 feet, 6 inches. The animal had been seriously crippled by the complete loss of both of its tail flukes, which may have been amputated by a ship's propeller. When it dove and thrust its mutilated tail-stump out of the water, as it did when approached, its identification was easy. Successive sightings indicate that it swam northward from San Diego to Alaska in 70 days. Estimating the distance covered at from 3,000 to 3,500 miles gives an average daily speed of 45 to 50 miles. The speed of the normal gray whale would be approximately 4 knots for 20 hours per day, or about 80 nautical miles a day (Gilmore, 1959).

The recognized champion with regard to speed of swimming is the dolphin. Pliny the Elder describes it as the swiftest of all animals, including even birds (Rackham, 1947, ix. 20). In mod-

5

ern times, claims of 50 to 75 miles per hour have been made for this animal. When swimming hard, it gives the illusion of going considerably faster than it actually is. Carefully clocked records of swimming speeds indicate how exaggerated these claims can be.

Townsend (1916) reported that bottlenose dolphins preceded his boat going at 12 miles per hour for one hour, and on another occasion at 15 miles per hour for two hours. Moore (1953, p. 137) chased a porpoise in a river with an outboard boat at 12.2 miles per hour. He thinks that the animal was frightened and was going at full speed. Gunter (1942, p. 269) saw dolphins overtake a speedboat going 22 miles per hour, and Remington Kellogg (1940) has reported a maximum speed of about 18 knots for the common dolphin, *Delphinus delphis*. Gunter believes this is about right for the bottlenose dolphin, *Tursiops truncatus*. "The fifty-mile-an-hour speed, for which they are given credit . . . is preposterous," he writes (Gunter, 1942, p. 269).

On many occasions, we have encountered small groups of bottlenose porpoises in a motorboat capable of speeds up to 28 miles per hour. Often we found that they would not approach the boat. The best method of attracting them to the bow, we discovered, was to set a course so as to go by the animals at a distance of 100 yards or so. We would then throttle down to about half speed (roughly 12 miles per hour)—a rate which finally became designated as "porpoise speed." The porpoises were much more likely to dash toward us and assume the desired position at the bow of the boat under these conditions than if we went too fast or too slow. A medium speed in this case was the most preferred or desirable one.

SKIN-WAVES IN SWIMMING

How are greater speeds, up to 20 or more miles per hour, possible? To force a dolphin through the water at such a rate would require more power than the animal apparently possesses.

6

An explanation in the form of increased muscular efficiency or reduced friction to the passage of the water would seem to be in order. But the muscular strength of whales and porpoises has been shown to be no greater per unit of volume than that of land-dwelling mammals (Ewer, 1947). Consequently, the explanation must lie in some special type of streamlining.

A solution to the problem is furnished by examining the skin of the porpoise's body. Essapian (1955) has shown that the skin of the trunk is loose and pliable. It may hang in folds or wrinkles if an animal is picked up and carried. The external layers of the skin also contain a multitude of tiny ducts which are filled with a spongy material (Kramer, 1960). As a result, the entire surface undulates in waves according to the turbulence or waviness of the water. The external shape of the animal, being somewhat flexible, assumes the natural contour of the flow of water which is rushing past it. Although at first glance it might appear that an uneven surface would generate more resistance than a smooth one, this is not so if the ripples coincide with the physical pressures of the water. The configuration of the skin matches the wave-form of the water, instead of opposing it. The result is known as "laminar flow." It has the effect of reducing friction drag by as much as 90 per cent over the friction of an unyielding surface (Kramer, 1960, p. 1118).

Some remarkable underwater photographs of the skin waves of live dolphins swimming at high speed have been made by Essapian (1955). He noted that the waves are at right angles to the direction of swimming and that they "are stationary and do not progress wave-fashion." This would be expected if they were turbulence waves produced by locomotion. Unlike the hull of a ship, a porpoise's body surface gives or adjusts in accordance with the pressure variations of the fluid around it.

In this instance, as in so many others, man has learned to improve his inventions by following what he sees in nature. By the encasing of steel submarines in undulating plastic skins, their passage through the water is made easier. As a conse-

7

quence, the speed of the vessel can be greatly increased without increasing the horsepower of the engines (Kramer, 1960).

SUBMARINE PORPOISE NOISES

A little-known fact about the bottlenose dolphin is that it makes many underwater noises. These sounds vary in intensity, in pitch or frequency, and in time of occurrence. Knowing this fact, one would naturally suspect that such water-borne noises must have some special significance.

Suppose at this point that we take a glimpse beneath the surface of the water at the sound-producing activity of these organisms. By way of illustration, we shall describe a specific incident which occurred in a small part of a comprehensive research program. This should give the reader some notion of what is to come and should serve as a brief introduction to the topics to be discussed in subsequent pages. The account, as written here, is taken from notes which were made immediately after the incident took place.

We were 2 miles off the north coast of Florida on the blue waters of the Gulf of Mexico. The white sands of the beach gleamed in the distance. A few feathery clouds were scattered here and there across the otherwise clear sky. I had just shut off the motor, and our boat—a gray Navy speedboat known technically as a "24-foot plane personnel boat"—was drifting in the light swell.

We had stopped because we had sighted a school of dolphins or porpoises playing or fishing about half a mile away. Our mission was to listen to the underwater noises made by free or wild porpoises in their natural state and if possible to obtain tape recordings of their sounds.

I lowered the Navy hydrophone—a special type of microphone for receiving submarine sound waves—and Robert Kohler, electronics engineer of the Oceanographic Institute of Florida State University, started our battery-operated d.c.-a.c.

8

inverter, adjusted the pre-amplifier, and connected the tape recorder which we carried in the boat. As the radio tubes warmed, the noises from beneath the surface of the sea—which are ordinarily inaudible to air-dwelling creatures like man—began to come from the loud-speaker in the cockpit of the boat. We could hear the lapping of the water upon the sides of the boat— louder and clearer when picked up under water than when heard directly in the air.

The porpoises had apparently noticed us, for their jumping and splashing ceased. They seemed to be making their way in our direction, although we could not be sure at that distance.

We listened intently at the speaker. At first we heard nothing but the usual water noise. But presently, between the slapping of the waves as the boat rolled gently back and forth, we thought we could detect a faint clicking or tapping, not unlike the pecking of a woodpecker. The sound grew slightly louder, and we strained our eyes at the bobbing dorsal fins of the porpoises across the water. They now seemed about one-quarter of a mile away. There could be no question that the animals were swimming toward us.

"Better turn on the tape recorder," I shouted to Bob. "We may get nothing, but this looks like too good a chance to miss."

The porpoises came straight in our direction. Soon we could see the smooth gray back beneath each triangular dorsal fin as the animals came up rhythmically for air and dove again in a graceful arc. The sunlight reflected from their glistening bodies.

There must have been nearly twenty in the group—a rather large number for this locality. When within 50 or 75 feet of our craft, they all submerged and swam directly beneath us. Looking down through the water, we could see dark shapes streaking swiftly past.

During all this time, the only noise we heard them make in the air was the "whoosh" of exhaling breath as their blowholes were momentarily out of water at the top of each arc—and

9

even this was audible only when they were close to the boat.

But the underwater listening gear told a very different story. The intermittent tapping or sputtering which had been barely discernible from the speaker when the animals first turned in our direction grew in intensity and in continuity as they approached. When emitted by a single porpoise alone, this noise— as we had learned before—is a concatenation of clicks or clacks such as might be produced by a rusty hinge if it were opened slowly. It was soon apparent, however, that a number of the animals were making the sounds together, and more seemed to join the chorus as they came nearer. Superimposed upon this increasing clatter was an occasional birdlike whistle resembling the "cheep" of a canary.

As they came still closer, the sputtering noises continued to grow louder and still louder. Taken together, they suggested the roar of an approaching railroad train, except perhaps that they were more irregular. By the time the group was about ready to make its final dive, the crescendo from the speaker in our boat had become a clattering din which almost drowned out the human voice.

Then abruptly, as if by prearranged signal, it stopped completely and left us in a shocking silence. At that moment, they swam beneath the boat. A single barklike sound was now repeated once or twice, and the porpoises with their underwater chorus were gone.

Never before that time—and never since—have we been fortunate enough to capture such an auditory event on magnetic recording tape. The weather had to be good. The sea had to be calm. We had to be out on the water in the right kind of boat. We had to have with us not only appropriate listening equipment but also a good recorder and a usable source of 110-volt current. The porpoises had to be present. And they had to choose to swim in our direction. It was a monumental piece of luck, perhaps not to be duplicated in a long time.

Chapter 2

The Amazing Dolphin

Animals which can be closely observed are often found to have consistent or predominant ways of behaving. Thus, we may speak of a horse as "docile" or as "spirited," or of a dog as "vicious" or "cowed." If such words accurately describe the traits or characteristics of an organism's behavior, they are not necessarily anthropomorphic. So we can refer with some sense to an animal's personality—meaning thereby its general patterns of activity. Applying this sort of terminology to the activity of porpoises or dolphins, one would say that they are generally pleasant and friendly.

ANCIENT RECORDS OF THE DOLPHIN

References to the behavioral or personality traits of the dolphin occur in very early writings. Its graceful form has also been found in the relics of ancient peoples who used it in wall paintings, on coins, and as decorations on vases. A pictographic seal from Crete is estimated to date from 3500 to 2200 B.C. (Stebbins, 1929, p. 19). Odysseus (*ca.* 900 B.C.) used the dolphin on his coat of arms (Haan, 1957). The particular animal which was admired in these distant times was undoubtedly the common dolphin of the Mediterranean, *Delphinus delphis*. Yet the similarity between the Mediterranean species and its relative, the bottlenose porpoise, is close enough to make the early descriptions applicable to either organism.

It is in Greek culture that the dolphin appears as a rescuer of drowning people. The classic fable of Arion is told by Herodotus in the sixth century B.C. (Godley, 1920, I, 24). On a ship bound from Corinth to Sicily, Arion was threatened by sailors who plotted to kill him for his money. He threw himself into the sea fully clothed and was saved by a dolphin which carried him to shore upon its back.

This theme of helping human beings in peril became very popular and was repeated so often that the animal finally became deified and was believed to accompany man "not only during life but also in death" (Haan, 1957, p. 10). In some places the image of the dolphin was regarded as sacred. The early Christians adopted it as a symbol which, in different contexts, served as a sign of several things—all of them good. For example, it represented "either the Lord Himself, the individual Christian, or abstract qualities such as those of swiftness, brilliancy, conjugal affection" (Smith and Cheetham, 1908, p. 571).

In Roman literature, the work of Pliny the Elder (A.D. 23–79) also extols the virtues of the dolphin. Pliny's *Natural History* contains several anecdotes of the friendship and love existing between young boys and porpoises. Somewhat apologetically he wrote, "I should be ashamed to tell the story were it not that it has been written about by Maecenas and Fabianus and Flavius Alfius and many others—and when the boy called to it at whatever time of day, although it was concealed in hiding it used to fly to him out of the depth, eat out of his hand, and let him mount on its back . . . and used to carry him when mounted right across the bay to Pozzuoli to school, bringing him back in a similar manner, for several years. . . . Another boy also, named Hermias, while riding across the sea in the same manner lost his life in the waves of a sudden storm, but was brought back to the shore, and the dolphin confessing itself the cause of his death did not return out to sea and expired on dry land" (Rackham, 1947, ix. 25 ff.).

Many other stories of a similar nature can be found in classical writings. A scholarly treatise by Stebbins (1929) describes existing records of the dolphin in the art and literature of Greece and Rome. A more general treatment of porpoises and of porpoise lore will be found in *A Book of Dolphins* by Antony Alpers (1960).

DO PORPOISES SAVE SWIMMERS?

Although accounts of the rescue by porpoises of drowning or worn-out swimmers are of ancient origin, they are not necessarily out of date. They are, in fact, current today and can be found the world over in seafaring and fishing centers. An example was published not long ago in the journal *Natural History* (1949). A mature, well-educated woman, who was walking waist deep in 2-foot waves about 10 feet from an ocean beach, was pulled down because of the undertow and was swept beneath the surface. She floundered, swallowed a great deal of water, and was unable to regain her footing.

Her statement continues, ". . . as I gradually lost consciousness . . . someone gave me a terrific shove, and I landed on the beach, face down, too exhausted to turn over. . . . It was several minutes before I could do so, and when I did, no one was near, but in the water about 18 feet out a porpoise was leaping around. . . .

"When I got enough energy to get back up the steps, a man who had been standing on the other side of the fence on the public beach came running over. . . . He said that when he had arrived, I looked like a dead body and that the porpoise shoved me ashore."

An even more recent account of porpoise assistance, which received wide publicity, was given early in 1960. Mrs. Yvonne M. Bliss of Stuart, Florida, aged 50 years, fell overboard, off the east coast of Grand Bahama Island in the West Indies. It was about 9:30 at night on February 29. There was no witness to the incident, so the information given cannot be corroborated. Following is an excerpt from her signed deposition.[1]

"After floating, swimming, shedding more clothing for what seemed to be an eternity, I saw a form in the water to the left of me. I thought it might be my jacket following along with the tide. Taking a better look I realized it was not the jacket, but some sort of sea life. It touched the side of my hip and thinking it must be a shark, I moved over to the right to try to get away from it. It took a great deal of concentration to keep from panicking. This change in position was to my advantage as heretofore I was bucking a cross tide and the waves would wash over my head and I would swallow a great deal of water. This sea animal which I knew by this time must be a porpoise had guided me so that I was being carried with the tide.

"After another eternity and being thankful that my friend was keeping away the sharks and barracuda for which these waters are famous, the porpoise moved back of me and came around to my right side. I moved over to give room to my companion and later knew that had not the porpoise done this, I would have been going down stream to deeper and faster moving waters. The porpoise had guided me to the section where the water was the most shallow.

"Shortly I touched what felt like fish netting to my feet. It was seaweed and under that the glorious and most welcome bottom.

"As I turned toward shore, stumbling, losing balance and saying a prayer of thanks, my rescuer took off like a streak on down the channel."

[1] Written for the author, after a personal interview.

PUSHING PORPOISE INFANTS

Surprisingly enough, a porpoise is born tail first, in a position reversed from that of land-dwelling mammals (Essapian, 1953). This is probably because it might drown if the blowhole were exposed before the baby could come to the surface for air. Newborn infants which do not rise for air at once are pushed to the surface by their elders. An injured adult may also be supported by an assisting pair of dolphins which swim on either side of it. Co-operation between several individuals takes place in such instances. There are well-authenticated observations which attest to this behavior (McBride, 1940; McBride and Hebb, 1948; McBride and Kritzler, 1951; Siebenaler and Caldwell, 1956).

There are also records of porpoises swimming at sea, carrying dead, mutilated, or decomposing porpoise babies on their backs in front of the dorsal fin, or on their heads (Hubbs, 1953; Moore, 1953, 1955). In one such case, the infant appeared to have been dead for days and so may have been carried for days. The carrying porpoise swam in an unusual manner, keeping its fin continuously out of the water. It did not dive with the other porpoises that accompanied it (Moore, 1955). This persistent, protective behavior seems to be a common characteristic of the dolphin. It is not inconceivable that, under the proper conditions, such activity could be applied to a human body.

RIDING A PORPOISE

Also of ancient origin is the notion of a porpoise being ridden like a horse. The image of a boy astride a dolphin is a familiar motif in classical art and sculpture and has been reproduced many times. It should be noted, however, that swimming with a human rider in an upright position is a very different thing from the spontaneous pushing of a floating body in the water. In fact, a basic principle of physics can be shown

15

to argue against the entire notion. For, if the porpoise made any forward progress—even at the top of the water so that a human swimmer could breathe—the water pressure or resistance against his legs and body would be perpendicular to the direction of movement. This would make it impossible to remain seated in an upright position upon the slippery torso of the animal. A much more reasonable method would be not to "ride," but to be pulled through the water. The swimmer could then grasp the triangular dorsal fin with his clasped hands, allowing his body to remain horizontal above that of the porpoise. The real problem in this instance would be to maintain a firm enough grip on the fin.

In spite of such academic arguments, there are records from both ancient and modern times which indicate that the riding of a porpoise like a horse has actually occurred. It has occurred, moreover, not as a trained act in a porpoise exhibit, but with wild or free-swimming animals. The entire procedure on the part of the animal appears to be spontaneous and voluntary. An almost unbelievable account, given in considerable detail, is reported by Pliny the Younger (Bosanquet, 1909, ix. 33).

"There is in Africa a town called Hippo, situated not far from the seacoast: it stands upon a navigable lake, communicating with an estuary in the form of a river, which alternately flows into the lake, or into the ocean, according to the ebb and flow of the tide. People of all ages amuse themselves here with fishing, sailing, or swimming; especially boys, whom love of play brings to the spot. With these it is a fine and manly achievement to be able to swim the farthest; and he that leaves the shore and his companions at the greatest distance gains the victory. It happened, in one of these trials of skill, that a certain boy, bolder than the rest, launched out towards the opposite shore. He was met by a dolphin, who sometimes swam before him, and sometimes behind him, then played round him, and at last took him upon his back, and set him down, and afterwards took him up again; and thus he carried the poor frightened fellow out into the deepest part; when immediately he turns back again to the shore, and lands him amongst his companions. . . .

"The next day the shore was thronged with spectators, all attentively watching the ocean, and (what indeed is almost itself an ocean) the lake. Meanwhile the boys swam as usual, and among the rest, the boy I am speaking of went into the lake, but with more caution than before. The dolphin appeared again and came to the boy, who, together with his companions, swam away with the utmost precipitation. The dolphin, as though to invite and call them back, leaped and dived up and down, in a series of circular movements. This he practised the next day, the day after, and for several days together, till the people (accustomed from their infancy to the sea) began to be ashamed of their timidity. They ventured, therefore, to advance nearer, playing with him and calling him to them, while he, in return, suffered himself to be touched and stroked. Use rendered them courageous. The boy, in particular, who first made the experiment, swam by the side of him, and, leaping upon his back, was carried backwards and forewards in that manner, and thought the dolphin knew him and was fond of him, while he too had grown fond of the dolphin. . . .

"It is very remarkable that this dolphin was followed by a second, which seemed only as a spectator and attendant on the former; for he did not at all submit to the same familiarities as the first, but only escorted him backwards and forwards, as the boys did their comrade."

This entire story can be shrugged off, if one wishes, as a fantastic tale of times gone by. If it is given any credence, however, there are two special features of it which are worthy of note. (1) The details recorded seem to be both logical and natural in the order or sequence in which they took place. (2) Only one porpoise engaged in this activity, the other remaining aloof or afraid.

THE DOLPHIN OF OPONONI

It may come as a shock to the skeptic to learn that this account written by Pliny 1,800 years ago is not without present-day support. In 1956, a similar event took place at the small seaside town of Opononi, in New Zealand. The New Zealand porpoise was named Opo—an abbreviation of the town that it made famous. It is known positively to have been a bottlenose dolphin.

". . . Unusually affable, even for a dolphin, Opo had approached the beach earlier in the season, began to frolic with a group of swimmers and was soon making daily visits to the resort. Opo proved particularly fond of the children. Swimming in close to the shore, she would wait for one of them to climb up on her back, then take off on a ride which usually ended in a friendly dunking. When the youngsters gathered for water games, Opo swam up and joined in the play, quickly became an expert at tossing a beach ball.

"Visitors flocked to Opononi to eye Opo, signs were posted nearby and legislation proposed to protect her. . . .

"Though Opo spent as many as six hours a day enjoying herself at the beach, other hours were devoted to seeking for food in the quiet bays along the coast. Nuzzling about one of them toward the end of the season, Opo became stranded on the rocks as the tide ran out. . . .

"Opononi went into mourning. All the stores closed for the day and flags were lowered to half-mast. Solemnly Opo was buried next to the returned soldiers' home and a New Zealand artist began sketches for a monument to commemorate the friendly dolphin of Opononi beaches." [2]

A more detailed description of the behavior of this people-loving animal, and of the crowds which came to see it, has

[2] Courtesy *Life* magazine, April 23, 1956, pp. 105–10. Copyright 1956 Time, Inc.

recently been given by Antony Alpers (1960, pp. 125–41). Alpers, who is a resident of New Zealand, has been able to assemble a series of photographs of the events which took place and has interviewed numerous persons who were first-hand participants. He gives the following statement by Jill Baker of Opononi, who was a particular favorite of the dolphin. Jill was thirteen years old when she encountered Opo, and she was an excellent swimmer.

"I think why the dolphin became so friendly with me was because I was always gentle with her and never rushed at her as so many bathers did. No matter how many went in the water playing with her, as soon as I went in for a swim she would leave all the others and go off side-by-side with me. I remember on one occasion I went for a swim much further up the beach than where she was playing, and I was only in the water a short while when she bobbed up just in front of my face and gave me such a fright. On several other occasions when I was standing in the water with my legs apart she would go between them and pick me up and carry me a short distance before dropping me again. At first she didn't like the feel of my hands and would dart away, but after a while when she realized that I would not harm her she would come to me to be rubbed and patted. She would quite often let me put little children on her back for a moment or two" (Alpers, 1960, p. 133).

In spite of the astonishing nature of these events, their authenticity can hardly be questioned. The following general inferences concerning them appear to be justified:

1. The entire activity appears to arise from a kind of playfulness.

2. It is engaged in only by exceptional porpoises and is by no means common to the species as a whole. This may explain the rarity of such events.

3. The "rides" (at least in the New Zealand case) did not last very long.

4. They began in shallow water—probably two or three feet —where a child could easily stand up.

5. The riding gradually evolved from repeated practice attempts.

6. The rider straddled the porpoise in front of (not behind) the dorsal fin.

7. Certain individuals, particularly children, seem to be preferred by the animal for such rides.

8. If all this is true, it follows that many of the dolphin accounts related by the ancients may well be correct, or at least have a real foundation in fact.

The strength and swimming power of the porpoise are certainly sufficient to take care of a human rider. This has been demonstrated in some unusual tests made by Mr. Adolph Frohm of the Miami Seaquarium. Mr. Frohm succeeded in harnessing a 30-pound bag of sand on the back of a captive porpoise. The harness was designed to support the sandbag in front of the dorsal fin. What had been thought might prove a severe handicap to the animal's motility actually disturbed it but little, for the porpoise appeared to swim easily under such a burden. In contrast to the weight of the sand, a human body when submerged in water has no weight at all—or practically none. Only that portion of the body which was out of the water would really have any weight. It would seem, therefore, that an adult porpoise can support a considerable portion of a rider's body above the water line.

DIVING WITH WILD PORPOISES

Opo, the dolphin of Opononi, would approach close enough to fishermen in outboard boats to permit them to touch it (Toi, 1958). But what would a free-swimming porpoise do if it encountered a group of strange divers beneath the surface of the water? The answer, I suspect, is that the typical porpoise would remain at least out of arm's reach. An interesting exception to this rule, however, has been described by Dr. Dean J.

Clyde, a research psychologist at the National Institute of Mental Health in Washington, D.C. Dr. Clyde lived for five years in the West Indies, where the water is very clear. During that time he became an ardent and skilful skin diver and SCUBA diver. In the spring of 1956—while under water off the northeast shore of St. Thomas, Virgin Islands—he and his companions were discovered by a group of porpoises. The following statement written by Dr. Clyde for this book, describes his experience.

"The rocky shore, consisting of huge boulders, dropped off suddenly under water to a depth of about one hundred feet. It continued to drop the further you got from shore to much greater depths. I was swimming with two others, equipped with an Aqualung, about 30 feet below the surface.

"A school of perhaps 15 porpoises of various sizes swam in among us from deeper water. They cavorted with us for 15 to 20 minutes. Quite a few of them (the smaller ones, as I recall) came close enough to me repeatedly so that I touched and even stroked them with my hand. They did not recoil when I did this. Then they swam away as suddenly as they had come.

"Although we usually saw quite a few sharks in this vicinity, on the day we encountered the porpoises we saw none at all."

TIMIDITY OR HESITANCY

It should be emphasized—in spite of these instances of voluntary physical contact and of porpoise riding—that such occurrences are rare and special events. They do not represent the usual behavior of wild or free-swimming dolphins. A dolphin in physical contact with a person is quite likely a dolphin which has gradually worked up to that stage. These animals will normally keep their distance when around human beings.

The timidity or hesitation of a young captive specimen as it swam close to a human attendant for the first time of its own choice is illustrated in the following excerpt from our laboratory notes. "It made a great to-do about coming after a fish held in the hand but did not have nerve enough to follow through. In fact, it behaved exactly like a little boy trying to make his first dive from a diving board. It would orient toward me, take a good look, and then surge forward with tremendous enthusiasm. But before it got close enough to make a pass at the fish, it would stop completely or else swim by two or three feet away. For about the first half of the feeding period there had not been a single successful approach, although the porpoise had made a great many starts. On the tenth or eleventh trial, it finally came in close enough to get its mouth on the fish."

ATTITUDE TOWARD MAN

Even though porpoises as a group do not seek wholesale physical contact with human beings, there is no denying the fact that they are very much interested in their land-dwelling friends. These animals are famous for their tendency to swim toward almost any boat or vessel that is near them. They will also come close to swimmers and divers, as we have seen. In this respect the dolphin is unique in that it appears to be what might be called "man-oriented." Instead of running at the sight of a person—like the timid creatures of the woods—it seems to seek proximity with human beings. Its attitude is even more friendly, perhaps, than that of the domesticated dog or horse. I have seen a porpoise swim back and forth inside an enclosure, keeping pace with a strolling person who walked back and forth on the dock beside it.

When captured or kept out of the water, porpoises remain perfectly quiet and do not thrash or struggle like fishes or sharks. They are commonly carried from place to place on a hospital stretcher or litter. When handled in this manner they co-operate fully and seem to be aware of what is going on. Their behavior seldom, if ever, appears to be senseless, hostile, or vicious.

A quotation from Plutarch, written centuries ago, beautifully describes this extraordinary attitude toward man. "To the dolphin alone, beyond all others, nature has granted what the best philosophers seek: friendship for no advantage. Though it has no need at all of any man, yet it is a genial friend to all and has helped many" (Cherniss and Helmbold, 1957, p. 473).

Porpoises are certainly engaging and delightful animals. Sailors have long regarded their presence about a ship as a good omen. Not only are they fascinating to watch in motion, but their streamlined forms are also attractive in repose. Even the mouth has a curvature which is often interpreted as a "built-in" smile, although the animal has no power of movement to produce a change in its contour.

OTHER INSTANCES OF PLAY

Without doubt, the porpoise's most common form of play is the familiar frolicking and leaping about the bows of moving boats or vessels. Woodcock (1948) was the first to note that in the course of this activity, a porpoise sometimes gets a free ride by "coasting down" the bow-wave. Riding the bow-wave of a ship at sea is a trick practiced only by dolphins or porpoises, although in theory it might also be done by other animals such as seals, manatees, walruses, or even fishes.

Just how is this maneuver accomplished? If a porpoise had weight, it could slide down the hill of water which is pushed forward by a ship's advancing prow. But the specific gravity of the animal is nearly the same as that of the water in which it swims. As a result, the downward pull of gravity would be insufficient to carry it along within the wave. The hydrodynamics of this form of activity are not completely understood, and several views of the forces involved are taken by different writers (Hayes, 1959; Scholander, 1959; Woodcock and McBride, 1951). It has even been noted that porpoises will "surf-ride" the incoming side of large breakers along a beach (Caldwell and Fields, 1959).

Porpoises in captivity will retrieve objects thrown to them and are easily taught to throw back these objects to human attendants on land. One animal, which was kept in a pen in the Bahama Islands, apparently invented a game of retrieving all its own. When no human beings were close by, it picked up a small floating stick about 8 inches long in its mouth and threw the stick forward for a distance of 10 feet or so. Then it swam ahead and picked up the stick, only to throw it again for another 10 feet. This sequence of activity was repeated as the animal swam around in a circle perhaps 50 feet across. Such behavior is apparently an instance of pure, spontaneous playfulness.

The way in which a group of porpoises reacts to a floating feather is aptly set forth in a statement by McBride and Hebb (1948, p. 116). We can do no better than to reproduce it here. "The individual porpoise finding a feather from one of the pelicans that inhabit the surface of the tank may come up, balance it on his nose out of water, flip it backward, try to catch it, and so on. Another is likely to come rushing up also and catch the feather as it falls and race off, pursued by others who try to take it from him. One may catch it out of the side of his mouth, the rest then pursuing the new owner of the prize. Such play among two or three of the porpoises may last an hour or more."

Dr. F. C. W. Olson, of the RCA Research Laboratories at Princeton, New Jersey, during a visit to captive porpoises at Marineland, Florida, observed an animal in what appeared to be an act of pure mischief. The porpoise gently seized the tail of a good-sized fish, swam *backward* holding the fish in its mouth for a distance of about 10 feet, and then released the fish unharmed. Since the porpoises in the tank were all well fed and never ate the live fishes swimming around them, the tail-pulling episode was interpreted as a case of fun-loving whimsy or teasing. Describing playful antics of a similar nature, Essapian (1953, p. 396) writes, "The most remarkable thing is that they play without any expectation of reward, simply for the pleasure of it." The playfulness of the porpoise may well exceed that of any other organism except *Homo sapiens.*

INTELLIGENCE

An accurate assessment of the intelligence and learning ability of this interesting animal is not yet possible because of the dearth of experimental research on the subject. The naturalistic and anecdotal evidence that could be cited is almost endless. A porpoise can do remarkable things, and man's opinion of this animal is generally of a high order and very favorable. Two important difficulties stand out in the attempt to equate the intelligence of porpoises with that of other animals. (1) The watery surroundings in which they live make it unusually difficult to study them. (2) They lack such manipulative or prehensile parts as hands or fingers. As a consequence, they are unable to work with levers, knobs, or mechanical apparatus like monkeys and apes. This does not necessarily mean that the intelligence of porpoises is inferior. It indicates only that proper comparisons cannot be made with manipulative problems.

Perhaps the best non-research evidence on this question is shown in the ease with which they can be trained for exhibition purposes and the surprising stunts they are capable of learning. At public exhibits at Marineland, Florida, at Miami, Florida, and at Palos Verdes Estates, California, porpoises stand on their tails, catch and throw balls and other objects, pull small boats or surfboards, jump through hoops, jump for objects held high in the air, "play basketball," "play baseball," and respond to many auditory and visual cues. To all appearances, they perform such learned activities with eagerness and enthusiasm.

A pertinent question in this regard is whether the porpoise is as intelligent as the anthropoid apes. Many comparative psychologists have regarded the chimpanzee or the gorilla as the most capable and advanced of all the animals. However, McBride and Hebb (1948) suggest that the chimpanzee has probably been overrated by students of this question. The intelli-

25

gence and learning ability of the bottlenose dolphin, in the opinion of these writers, may actually place it as high or higher than apes in any comparative ranking.

Support for this position is furnished by the recent work of Dr. John C. Lilly of the Communication Research Institute at St. Thomas in the Virgin Islands. Implanting electrodes in the so-called pleasure and pain centers of the brain, Lilly trained porpoises to push a lever with their noses either to switch on or to switch off an electric current. Naïve monkeys require several hundred trials to master a trick like this, but one of Lilly's porpoises did it in twenty trials. Another, in a slightly different situation, is reported to have learned in five trials (Lilly, 1958). It is doubtful if a human subject could do better.

THE SIZE OF THE BRAIN

A somewhat different approach to the qestion of porpoise ability can be made through the study of brain structure. Since the nerve centers control both sensitivity and behavior, a large and complex brain indicates advanced capacities and potentialities. This principle does not hold between individuals of the same species, but it is a rough rule of thumb which can be applied from one species to another.

A good average weight for the brain of a fully grown dolphin is 1,600 grams, or about 3.5 pounds.[3] The brain of a 150-pound man, on the other hand, would weigh somewhere near 1,400 grams, or 3.1 pounds. At first glance, these values appear to rank man below the porpoise, but they leave out of account a very important factor. Because a full-grown porpoise is larger and heavier than a human being, its brain controls more body tissue than a human brain. A common way of allowing for this dis-

---

[3] Of seven dolphins examined by Kruger (1959), the four largest had an average brain weight of 1,625 grams or 3.6 pounds. Their body lengths averaged 8 feet, 1 inch. Two others were somewhat smaller and evidently immature. No figures were given for the seventh.

crepancy is to divide the brain weight of the organism by its total body weight. This gives the percentage of the body weight which is taken up by the brain.

TABLE 1

BRAIN WEIGHTS OF PORPOISE, CHIMPANZEE, AND MAN

Organism	(1) Body Wt. (Lb.)	(2) Brain Wt. (Lb.)	(2/1) Brain Wt. Body Wt. (per cent)	(3) Body Length (Ft.)	(2/3) Brain Wt. Body Length
Man	150	3.1	2.1	5.8	0.53
Porpoise ...	300	3.5	1.17	8.0	0.44
Chimpanzee	110	0.77	0.70	4.5	0.17

These and other calculations are brought together in Table 1 —for man, for the porpoise, and for the chimpanzee. The figures for body weights, heights, and brain weights in this table were chosen to represent a kind of median or typical value for each species. We see from such data that the brain of a human being constitutes about 2.1 per cent of the total weight of his body. The porpoise has 1.17 per cent of its weight in brain tissue, and the chimpanzee 0.70 of 1 per cent.

Dividing the brain weight by the height or length of the organism gives the number of pounds of brain tissue for each foot of body length. This is another, and perhaps better, way of indicating the degree of brain control over the body. A comparison like this—although necessarily crude—again shows the porpoise to be far ahead of the chimpanzee (see Table 1).

Still a third method of comparing different organisms in terms of neural structure is to examine the relative sizes of the spinal cord in relation to the brain. This would indicate the extent to which the higher centers of the central nervous system dominate the lower centers. A large brain in proportion to the spinal cord would consequently imply the development of more complex psychological functions. Such a method has been advocated by Carlson and Johnson (1953, p. 444) as the best of the neuroanatomical procedures for inferring intellectual ability. However, a possible error exists in this technique when comparing porpoises with terrestrial organisms like chimpanzees or man. The presence or absence of the hind limbs would quite likely act as an uncontrolled factor affecting the nerve distribution in the cord (Cunningham, 1877; Breathnach, 1960).

A NEUROTIC PORPOISE

Experiments on research animals, including rats, cats, dogs, and sheep, have shown that they can be made neurotic by certain laboratory methods. Under stressful or unusual conditions, other animals may also behave abnormally, as, for example, when an elephant "goes berserk." Does the friendly porpoise ever become similarly disturbed? Although it learns rapidly, is intelligent, playful, and interested in human beings, will it under some circumstances also display neurotic behavior?

A case of abnormal activity which could well be described in these terms occurred with a captive porpoise at the Florida State University Marine Laboratories. At one end of the pool where two research animals were kept were a couple of smaller enclosures or cages, 15 by 25 feet in size. These were constructed of wire fencing and of heavy war-surplus plastic. Each had an underwater door which also extended well above the water line. In the attempt to get a porpoise into one of these compartments, several methods were used. At first we tried to lure the animals with food-fish offered at the doorway. But they soon caught on and would not be tricked by this procedure. The only method that really worked was to float a steel net behind the individual to be caged so as to force it through the entrance.

Both our porpoises were successfully separated in this manner, but the effects of the procedure in the case of Betty—a sophisticated female—were both unfortunate and persistent. Betty was maneuvered into one of the compartments several times, and in one instance remained there for forty-eight hours. While in the cage, she tolerated petting and handling by persons who went into the water beside her, and at first she took food readily from the hand.

The space was quite confining, however, and Betty soon developed a kind of up-and-down motion without going anywhere. This was soon characterized by those present as "the rocking-horse movement." Her tail thrusts, which would normally have pushed her forward, were apparently counterbalanced by simultaneous backward movements of the flippers. The net result was to keep her always in the same position. Moreover, she went up and down at a faster rate than was necessary for breathing. This was shown by the fact that she usually took a breath only on every fourth or fifth rise of the rocking-horse movement.

What we did not realize at the time was that the caging technique, together with the feeding in the cage, had apparently constituted what amounted to an approach-avoidance situation for this animal. Eventually, she refused to accept any food at all, and so we transferred her back to the larger pool.

From that time onward, Betty would never consistently take food-fish from the hands of any of her human associates. Not only that, but the rocking-horse movement remained a regular part of her repertoire even after she had been released from the cage. This activity was particularly apparent whenever we tried to break down her resistance by tempting her with food-fish. She would swim to within 5 or 10 feet of the feeder and remain there, eyeing him as she rocked rhythmically up and down. On more than one occasion she came close, *then turned her back on the attendant,* and began her rocking routine.

As a result of Betty's abnormal behavior, unwittingly produced by her keepers, we were never able to use her in experiments in which positive reinforcement was the motivation. She refused completely to co-operate for a food reward and could be made to work only by negative reinforcement or punishment. She seemed to be telling us in no uncertain terms that we were no longer her friends.

CO-OPERATIVE FEEDING

In spite of this, she had to eat. And so, after this abrupt change in her activity, Betty got her food in other ways. The most common method she used was to eat fish which were thrown into the water nearby. But the second method was striking and unusual: she ate food-fish which Albert, her porpoise companion, had previously accepted from human hands, but which he himself had subsequently failed to swallow.

The male porpoise was much younger than Betty and appeared to be devoted to her. He successfully withstood the travail of the confinement and continued to behave normally in spite of it. Whether the fish which she received from him were the result of deliberate co-operation between the two we cannot say, of course, with certainty. But all observers agreed that it looked that way. Even at the beginning of a feeding session, when neither porpoise had eaten for several hours, Albert would frequently relinquish his food-fish to Betty.

He would take a fish in his mouth, both porpoises would disappear beneath the surface, and Betty would presently reappear with the fish in her mouth. It could not have been an accident for it occurred too many times. And there was never any fighting, splashing, or violent swimming involved. This looks like a case of concerted action in which individuals work together for a common end. In this respect it resembles the joint care of the newborn porpoise infant, which has been previously mentioned, or the riding of porpoises by human beings.

INDIVIDUAL DIFFERENCES

With regard to their general characteristics, these two porpoises were very different. Betty was independent, self-sufficient, and calm. She was less active and less aggressive in her movements. Her whole demeanor gave the impression of maturity and experience. In age, she must have been well along toward the porpoise's estimated life expectancy of thirty years.

Albert, on the other hand, could not have been over four or five years old. He displayed the typical energy of the adolescent. He was a great deal more playful and more active. Not infrequently he played with Betty by leaping over her, swimming around her in circles, or getting beneath her and pushing her partly out of the water. All this nonsense she seemed to tolerate with a kind of maternal reserve. Albert was more easily frightened and swam rapidly to her side in times of excitement or stress, as when a thunderstorm came up. At the same time, he was more adaptable than she; and he did not develop abnormal behavior.

Chapter 3

Sounds beneath the Sea

The oceans cover nearly three-quarters of the earth to an estimated average depth of about 13,000 feet. They are teeming with life of all kinds. Yet what goes on in these unexplored regions is one of the greatest mysteries with which man is faced. In some ways, he knows less about it than he does about the stars—for at least he can *see* them. Under water, the most important avenue for scientific investigation—namely, the use of visual observation—is either impossible or limited to a very small area close to the observer.

EXPLORING BY EAR

With the development of the science of electronics, a new technique for investigating the mysteries of the deep began to evolve. This was the method of *listening* to what took place beneath the surface of the water. If a man could not see what went on, he could at least hear and record the sounds that occurred. He could now grope about by sound, like a blind man, whereas before that time he had been both blind and deaf. This method of listening at the surface for noises generated in the ocean has developed more and more, until it has become one of the most important and exciting ways of getting oceanographic information.

The familiar idiom, "silent as the sea," is now known to be inaccurate and inappropriate. In certain places and under certain conditions, the waters of the ocean are alive with the noises of fishes, crabs, shrimp, and other organisms. This seems to be particularly true close to shore or where the water is not too deep. In the vast majority of such cases, a man listening in the air would not hear any of this.

For accurate underwater listening, special equipment is necessary. The technique requires the use of a hydrophone, or underwater microphone, appropriate electronic pre-amplifiers and amplifiers, and a suitable air speaker if the sounds are to be heard as they occur (Morris, Kohler, and Kellogg, 1953). When such listening is done from small boats—as is often the case—the source of electric current to operate the apparatus sometimes presents a problem. The best observations are made by testing captured specimens in salt-water tanks or aquariums in which disturbing background sounds and residual water noise can be eliminated.

IMPORTANCE OF THE PROBLEM

During World War II, the problem of noisemaking in the ocean rose from relative obscurity to great importance. At that time, the method of detecting the presence of enemy ships by listening for their engine and propeller sounds began to be used. Not only were submarines equipped with the necessary apparatus to do this, but installations were also placed at important harbors along the coast to guard against the entrance of enemy vessels.

Listening equipment of this sort was set up during the winter of 1942 at Fort Monroe to protect the entrance to Chesapeake Bay, and was found on the whole to work well as a detecting

33

device. In the spring, however, the loud-speakers at the stations on shore began to give off a concatenation of hammering noises resembling a chorus of pneumatic drills breaking up concrete pavement. In the evening, particularly, this became so voluminous that it drowned out completely any ship or propeller noises. Experts in acoustics who were rushed to the scene finally discovered that the noises were made by schools of croakers returning to the bay after spawning in the ocean (Loye and Proudfoot, 1946).

Similar incidents were reported by Navy vessels. The log of the United States submarine "Permit" contains the following entry: "0810. Sound picked up unusual noise . . . could see nothing through periscope on that bearing. This noise sounded like hammering on steel in a non-rhythmic fashion. . . ." There were corresponding records from other ships (Fish, 1954*b*). Such reports had a profound effect on the design of acoustic mines and torpedoes which were supposed to be detonated by the underwater noises of enemy vsesels. Perhaps the noises made by fishes could explode these devices!

Problems of this sort immediately initiated an intensive study of the sounds made by any marine noisemaker that could be identified. In this way, the animal noises could be recognized and discounted by trained observers, and electronic receiving equipment could be redesigned to filter out many of the undesirable sounds. The extent to which this research has progressed is shown by the bibliographies of published scientific reports on underwater noise of biological origin (W. Kellogg, 1953*a*; Moulton, 1960). One of these contains over 1,200 references, almost all of which deal with the sounds made by marine forms (Moulton, 1960).

Generally speaking, the kinds of sounds emitted by the fishes and marine *Crustacea* would be described by such terms as clicks or clacks, croaks, grunts, rattles, or thumps. The investigation of such noises is now a highly specialized field in itself and could well be made the subject of a book in its own right.

PLATE I. A porpoise which has just been captured in a net. Note graceful body-lines and horizontal tail flukes.

PLATE II. Mother and infant inhale before submersion. The blowholes can be seen to be open in each instance. (Courtesy Marine Studios.)

Plate III. Underwater photograph shows animals examining a hydrophone which was submerged in order to pick up their sounds. (Courtesy Marine Studios.)

PLATE IV. Porpoise swimming near a model of the 1K transducer (or underwater speaker) which broadcasts sounds into the water. (Courtesy Marine Studios.)

PLATE V. Apparatus used for analyzing porpoise sounds. The equipment shown here produced the photographs of echo-ranging pulses in Plate VIII. (1) Audio-amplifier. (2) Loud-speaker. (3) Oscilloscope camera. (4) Cathode-ray oscilloscope. (5) Audio-oscillator (for calibration). (6) Band-pass filter. (7–7') Ampex tape recorder from which porpoise noises are sent to oscilloscope. (8) Auxiliary recorder.

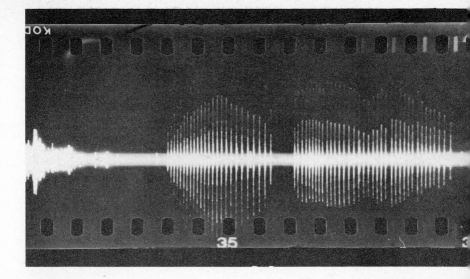

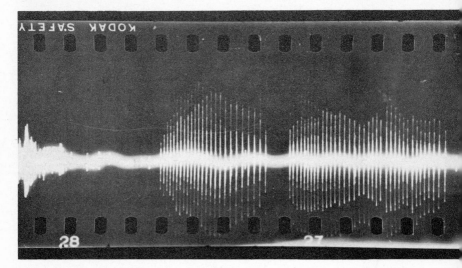

PLATE VI. Oscilloscopic photographs of porpoise clicks or sound pulses used in echo-ranging. (*Top*) Filmstrip showing a brief train of porpoise clicks beginning about a half-second after a surface splash. Several harmonics are indicated by the different densities of the spikes. The noise of the splash is shown at the left of the film. The clicks in this picture were photographed live as the porpoise made them. (*Bottom*) The same train of sound-pings photographed from the play-back of Ampex magnetic tape. The two pictures will be seen to be identical except for a slight AC modulation in the base line of the lower photograph.

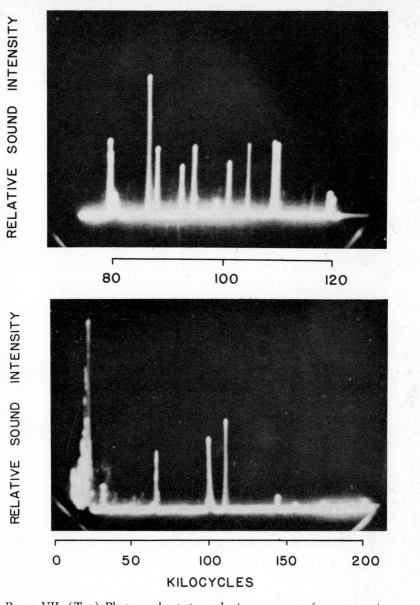

PLATE VII. (*Top*) Photograph ot the cathode-ray screen of a panoramic ultrasonic analyzer, showing frequency components occurring between 80 and 120 kc. in a series of porpoise clicks. Separate pips represent coincidence of the sweep of the cathode-ray tube with different clicks. Twelve clicks that occurred during the photographic exposure (0.5 sec. in this instance) thus contained frequencies extending at least to 120 kc. (*Bottom*) Photograph of the cathode-ray tube of the panoramic analyzer when the tuning range was 10–200 kc. The strongest frequencies, so far as intensity is concerned, will be seen to lie below 25 kc., but the short pips at the right indicate the presence of frequencies of 140, 155, and 170 kc., respectively.

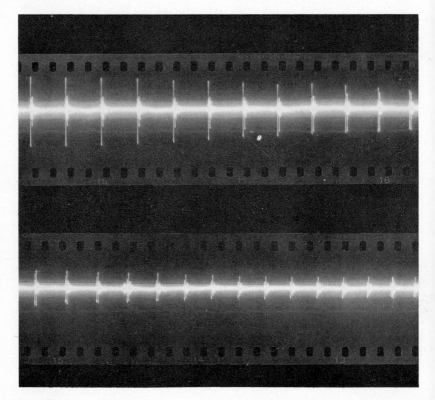

PLATE VIII. A series of clicks expanded laterally on this 35-mm. filmstrip so as to show echoes. The large vertical spike represents the original pulse, and the secondary spike immediately to the right of each pulse is its echo.

In this chapter we shall attempt only a brief survey of the problem as a prelude for what is to come later.

THE NOISES OF CRABS AND SHRIMP

Among the *Crustacea,* the most common—and in some ways the most annoying—of the noise producers is a tiny snapping shrimp. The snapping shrimp is inedible and has no commercial value. This little creature—smaller than one's little finger—possesses a claw like that of a lobster which it opens and closes to produce a kind of tapping or ticking sound. When large numbers of snapping shrimp sound off together, as is inevitably the case, the underwater crepitation produced is like static in a radio. It drowns out or masks many of the other underwater noises. Snapping shrimp occur throughout the oceans of the world between approximately latitudes 35 degrees north and 35 degrees south. Their sounds were first examined and identified by Martin Johnson (Johnson, 1944; Johnson, Everest, and Young, 1947).

Some crabs also make cracking or popping noises which are more sporadic and much louder than those of the snapping shrimp. The human observer, listening to these noises, might compare the background sounds of the snapping shrimp to the rifle fire of a regiment of infantry soldiers. The louder cracks or crunches of the crabs seem to stand out above this background noise like occasional mortar or artillery fire.

SOUNDS OF FISHES

As for the fishes themselves, it has long been recognized by anglers that some kinds of fish make sounds in the air after they have been caught. The popular names given certain species —grunt, drumfish, croaker, toadfish, and the like—are verbal evidence of this. But making noises in the air, it should be pointed out, may be a different thing from making noises while swimming freely in the water. Many fishes, so far as is known, produce no sounds of any kind. There is the mullet, for exam-

35

ple—a valuable food-fish—which could be accurately described as "silent as a fish." Research, on the other hand, has shown that such varying forms as the cowfish (W. Kellogg, 1955) and the sea horse (Fish, 1954*a*) emit characteristic noises in water.

Most of the sounds which fishes make, like those of the *Crustacea,* are of the percussion variety. That is, they are thumps or ticking or grinding sounds. The separate pulses, units, or "syllables" of such fish noises are therefore mostly of short duration. Some fishes, on the other hand, emit noises with a definite tonal quality which last for a longer time. Among them the cowfish, the sea catfish, and the toadfish appear to be the best noisemakers.

THE "LANGUAGE" OF THE TOADFISH

The most characteristic utterance of the toadfish resembles somewhat the croaking of a frog. It can be described as a kind of low-frequency, tonal "honk" or "boop." Other descriptive terms are the "boat-whistle" noise (Fish, 1954*a*) or the "foghorn" sound (Tavolga, 1960). In many cases, there is also a shorter, almost toneless "bup" which is frequently combined with the tonal syllable. An analysis of 273 toadfish sound patterns recorded at the Marine Laboratories of Florida State University on the Gulf Coast shows some unusual relationships. The hydrophone was located in about 5 feet of water in a muddy estuary, and the recordings were made in two separate sessions on different days.

The total length of a sound pattern or "word" on these recordings was found to vary from less than 1 second to more than 2 seconds, depending on the number of units it contained. The average interval between successive sound patterns was about 18 seconds, with a maximum of 1 minute, 40 seconds.

If dots are used to represent "bups" and dashes to represent "honks," the five words in the toadfish vocabulary—as they occurred in this situation—may be represented as: one dot, two dots, three dots, dot dash, and two-dots dash. A frequency tabulation of the five sound patterns is given in Table 2.

TABLE 2

FREQUENCY OF OCCURRENCE OF RECORDED SOUND PATTERNS
OF THE TOADFISH

Type of response	I	2	3	4	5	All Types
Sound combinations	.	. .	. . .	. —	. . —	
First recording day	26	4	0	22	14	63
Second recording day	145	32	3	27	0	207
Total	171	36	3	49	14	268

Perhaps the most interesting thing about such data is the relationship shown between the number and size of the units in a sound pattern and the frequency of its appearance. The longer in duration a particular combination of noises, the less often it takes place. Some indication of the reliability of these determinations can be found by comparing the order of the frequencies for the dot words and the dot-dash words on the two recording days.

It would appear that we have here an example of the Law of Least Effort, which is a well-known aspect of human speech. There is a negative relationship in written and spoken language between the length of a word and the frequency of its use. Zipf (1949) has pointed out that this rule holds for English, for Western European languages, for Chinese, for Latin, and for the languages of the American Indians. The same rule, at least in the present instance, seems also to hold for the toadfish.

SIGNIFICANCE OF THE SOUNDS

Since fishes have no vocal cords, they cannot produce noises in this way. Some possess grinding or pharyngeal teeth and make sounds by rubbing the teeth together, even though they are not eating. Other fishes emit sounds by means of the swim-bladder and have special drumming muscles which are rubbed against the bladder to produce the sound. Fish noises appear in some instances to be associated with breeding or spawning, in others to be defensive or protective. A number of fishes when squeezed, poked with a stick, or shocked with electricity will give off their "fishy" utterances. The noises produced under these conditions might almost be considered emotional, although such an interpretation, of course, is highly speculative.

Many fish sounds, it is clear, have no significance whatever. A case in point is that of the parrot fish, which has a powerful bonelike beak with which it scrapes or chews live coral from coral rock. The noises it makes doing this have a rasping or filing quality and are only incidental to eating (W. Kellogg, 1955).

The acoustical characteristics and frequency spectra of several fish noises have been worked out by Loye and Proudfoot (1946), Dobrin (1947), and Tavolga (1960). Many more have been analyzed by Dr. Marie P. Fish and her associates (Fish, Kelsey, and Mobray, 1952; Fish, 1954*a*, 1954*b*). Dr. Fish has also dealt with the mechanisms by which fishes are able to produce their sounds, as well as with the probable significance of these noises. A report by Japanese investigators discusses particularly those sea forms whose sounds contain ultrasonic wave lengths. The sounds of the spiny lobster, the hermit crab, and the filefish fall into this category (Japan. Fisheries Agency, 1958).

FISHING BY LISTENING

Both commercial and lay fishermen have recognized the possibilities of locating fishes by means of their noises, and numerous efforts have been made to employ this method in the fishing industry. There are difficulties with the method, however. In the first place, some of the most important food-fish do not conveniently broadcast self-directing sound signals. In the second place, those that do so, do not make the sounds regularly or dependably. Generally speaking, fish sounds follow a diurnal cycle and are louder in the evening than they are at other hours of the day.

The appearance of large schools of fishes which migrate in the spring of the year might be detected by semipermanent lisening stations in the general pathway of their migration. The Japanese have proposed that commercial fishing vessels set out "sonobuoys" to locate schools of fishes (Japan. Fisheries Agency, 1959). The sonobuoy is a floating device consisting of a hydrophone and radio transmitter. The reception of its signals by the fishing boat would require a radio receiver, a loud-speaker, and possibly a pen recorder. American manufacturers have recently put on the market a small hydrophone with earphones, called a "Fishfone," with which the individual small-boat fisherman can do his own listening.

The reverse method has also been tried. Noises have been transmitted into the water for the purpose of directing or steering fish in a particular direction, as for example, into a net. In every instance, the results of such tests have been negative (Moulton and Backus, 1955). An exceptionally thorough investigation, using fresh-water rainbow and brown trout, was undertaken by the Fish and Wildlife Division of the Department of the Interior (U.S. Fish and Wildlife Service, 1953). Four kinds of underwater sound generators broadcast frequencies from 67 to 70,000 cycles per second into a 450-foot pond. The distribution of fishes in the enclosure was unaffected by noises of any of the frequencies or intensities which could be produced.

Although the swimming of fishes is not affected by sound, the underwater noises of large schools of croakers can be momentarily silenced by small explosions. Yet, after a very brief interval, the chorus starts again with undiminished volume (Loye and Proudfoot, 1946). In the case of the sea robin, Moulton (1956) believes that artificial tones transmitted into the water can both stimulate and suppress its call. Fishes can be trained by the conditioned-reflex method to react to audio-vibrations in water, even though they do not respond to such stimuli before conditioning (Harlow, 1939; Kellogg and Spanovick, 1953). This shows that their indifference to vibratory stimuli is not due to an inability to sense them. The frog also has been found to remain immobile in a noisy environment (Yerkes, 1905).

The common notion that noises made in a fishing skiff will frighten away the fish may, therefore, be far from correct. A subsurface illustration of this point appeared in our research work when it became necessary to build some apparatus under water. The work required the use of ordinary carpenter's tools, such as a saw and a hammer, and was done at the end of a 300-foot dock in a small bay in the Gulf of Mexico. The builder was weighted down with a lead belt and was supplied with air through a compressed-air pump and a diving helmet. Even though the water was not very deep, the metallic sounds made by striking a heavy spike with a hammer must have carried well over a mile beneath the surface.

At one time, numerous angelfish happened to be in the vicinity. Far from fleeing at the auditory disturbance, they almost interfered with the operation by getting between the carpenter's face glass and the nail he was trying to hit. Neither the sounds nor the rhythmic arm movements made in hammering appeared to have any effect on their swimming behavior.

SOUND WAVES IN WATER

It might be well before leaving this subject to point out that the propagation of sound in water differs in many respects from the propagation of sound in air. Sound waves travel about five times as fast in sea water as they do in air, or at the rate of approximately one mile per second. Correspondingly, the length of a sound wave of any given frequency is approximately five times as long in water as it is in air. The transmission of sound in water is affected by temperature variations in the water, by depth or pressure, by the amount and character of the sediment, and by the degree of salt concentration or salinity (Gutenberg, 1960).

Since sound vibrations in water are reflected both downward from the surface and upward from the bottom, they tend to be confined pretty much within the sea. Noises made under water are not easily transmitted into the air because of the greater compressibility of the air. A sound produced in water can consequently reach a given point some distance away by several different pathways. An obvious path is the direct one from the source to the receiver. Or the path may be from the source to the bottom, and then to the receiver. More complex paths, such as source to surface, to bottom, to receiver, are also possible. When the surface and the bottom are close together, as in coastal waters, the multiplicity of reverberations rapidly attenuates the horizontal intensity. The over-all effect is somewhat like that produced by the baffle plates inside the muffler of an automobile.

If the sea surface and the bottom are rough, the sounds reflected from them will be garbled. Or, if the bottom is of soft mud, absorption takes place and the reflections will be reduced. Sound reflection and absorption characteristics also vary according to wave length, especially in the case of high ultrasonic frequencies (Japan. Fisheries Agency, 1955, 1956).

However, all such factors are of minor importance when the water is very deep. Under such circumstances, the distances which sound waves will travel are phenomenal. The noise of an underwater explosion made in the waters off Hawaii can be picked up some 40 minutes later by hydrophones in San Francisco. Moreover, the explosion does not need to be a very large one. Four pounds of TNT exploded at a depth of 4,000 feet will produce a disturbance which can be indentified at a distance of 10,000 miles (Ewing and Worzel, 1948).

This property of sound transmission in deep water is used by our Navy and Air Force to locate missiles which have landed in the ocean. An explosive charge in the missile is detached upon impact with the water and sinks to a prescribed depth before detonating. Hydrophones on ships in the vicinity can determine its approximate position by the direction and intensity of the sound waves. The method is known in the vernacular of the Navy as *SO*und *F*ixing *A*nd *R*anging (SOFAR).

Chapter 4

Indications of
Porpoise Sonar

Porpoises, as we have seen, are fast-swimming animals. The giant whales, although not so swift, possess tremendous mass. In both cases, the momentum of the organism, which is the product of its mass times its velocity, is great. As a consequence, a collision with a submerged obstacle—such as a rock or the bottom of a ship—would be disastrous. Obviously, these animals must have some means of detecting obstructions in their pathway. They must have a method of perceiving solid objects at a distance that will permit them to avoid such objects while swimming.

VISUAL PERCEPTION IN SEA WATER

One naturally thinks of the eye in this connection, since this is the primary organ of distance perception in man. One complicating factor for the whales and porpoises is that their eyes are set far on either side of the head. This means, according

43

to Langworthy (1932, p. 444), "that there is no opportunity for binocular stereoscopic vision." In another paper ·(1931*b*, p. 230) he says, "It has been clearly shown by one observer that, in the dolphin at least, all the optic fibres decussate in the midline so that there are no arrangements in the central nervous system for anything more complicated than panoramic vision." Panoramic vision would not be nearly as good for the accurate perception of objects at a distance as stereoscopic vision.

The matter is further complicated by the nature or structure of the eye. If each eye has a fovea, and if the fovea is toward the back of the retina as it is in fishes, there still might be stereoscopic vision. It could only exist, however, if there was overlapping of the visual fields. Some overlapping may occur in the visual fields of the porpoise on either side of the median line. This would be due in part to the refraction of the light waves as they pass from the water into the cornea. But in the case of the sperm whale, the enormous protuberance of the nose or snout would seem to preclude such a possibility.

Aside from this somewhat debatable point, there are physical reasons why vision does not work well in water—no matter how efficient the optical organ. For one thing, sea water often contains a large amount of sediment or silt. The sediment can be stirred up from the bottom by waves and currents, or it can be carried many miles into the ocean by great rivers. The water may also be filled with clouds of micro-organisms or plankton which—like fog on land—would drastically limit the range of vision.

In bright sunlight, even in the clearest ocean water, the distance from which an object can be detected is extremely short when compared to the miles we see on land. Backhouse (1960, p. 28) appropriately described the situation as follows. "Although whales and dolphins make use of their eyes when convenient, for much of the time especially in dark or murky waters, vision is of little value. Except in brilliant sunlight and

44

very clear water, visual range is so short as to be relatively valueless." Yet the whales and porpoises swim at night, when the penetration of light into the water is reduced much more. How can we account for this?

The bottlenose dolphin in particular is a frequent visitor to harbors, bays, and estuaries, where the water may be so turbid that visibility is limited to a few inches. Moreover, a big harbor contains both moving and anchored ships, buoys, piling, docks, and piers. How can a porpoise navigate amid such hazards, even in the daytime, without the risk of damaging or fatal accidents?

DIVING TO GREAT DEPTHS

Quite beyond and aside from these considerations is the matter of light penetration into the deeper regions of the sea. Because of the filtering effect of the water, the greater the depth, the darker it gets. William Beebe (1931, 1934), from his bathysphere, graphically described the step-by-step fading of the different spectral colors until ". . . the last hint of blue gradually tapers into a nameless gray, and this into black" (1931, p. 676). This phenomenon was observed again by Piccard in the dives of the bathyscaphe. Below approximately 1,000 feet, even on a perfect day, there is no light whatever, but only complete and permanent darkness (Piccard, 1956, p. 117).

The dolphin probably does not descend to 1,000 feet, but certain of the great whales are known to go far deeper. Old whaling records show that large sperm whales sometimes dived to a depth of three lines—a "line" being 220 fathoms in length (Bennett, 1840, p. 206). This means that a harpooned animal could go down more than 3,900 feet. More recent evidence that sperm whales swim well below half a mile was furnished by the United States cable repair ship, "All America," in 1932. Investigating an interruption in cable service between the Canal Zone and Ecuador, the vessel hauled to the surface a dead 45-ton sperm whale that had become caught in the submarine

45

cable at a depth of 3,240 feet. One hundred and eighty feet of cable were entwined about the lower jaw, one flipper, and the body of the animal (R. Kellogg, 1940, p. 37).

By what means at such depths does a whale find out when it is approaching the bottom? What prevents it from committing suicide by crashing its enormous bulk into the solid but invisible floor beneath it?

NAVIGATION WITHOUT VISION

Man has a method, which he is still perfecting, for navigation beneath the surface of the ocean without the use of vision. This is the method of sonar or echo-ranging. The word "sonar" is a contraction of the phrase so(und) n(avigation) a(nd) r(anging). The principle of sonar is the same as that of radar

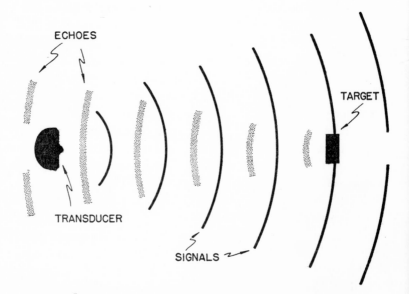

Fig. 1.—Diagram illustrating the general principle of the reflection of echoes in active sonar. The original pings of the signal can be non-directional, but if the reflecting target is small, the echoes will be returned from a specific point in space.

(radio direction and ranging), except that the distance and the speed of the acoustical echoes are much more limited than those of radio. Since radar will not work in water and vision is of little use for submarine navigation, sonar takes the place of both beneath the surface of the ocean.

In the application of the method, a train of repeated sound signals or pings is emitted by an underwater transducer. These are usually of high audio-frequency or are ultrasonic. Echoes from the pings are reflected back to the source from targets or submerged objects. The echoes are then electronically translated to give both the distance and, to some extent, the shape of the echoing target.[1]

Sonar is the fundamental method of navigation for a submarine operating beneath the surface. Used as a fathometer, or echo-sounder, the signals are beamed downward; they then indicate the depth and contour of the bottom. Used commercially as a "fish-finder," a sonar apparatus can detect the presence of schools of fishes by the echoes they reflect—regardless of whether the fish make any noises of their own.

THE ECHOLOCATION OF BATS

For some years, it has been known that a method like sonar is employed by bats flying in the dark. They emit a succession of high-pitched cries and control their direction of flight by analyzing the echoes. Probably, they even find the flying insects which they eat in this manner. In the case of the bat, however, the term "sonar" has not been extensively used, but "echolocation" seems to be preferred, largely because of the comprehensive work of Griffin (1958), who has popularized this term.

Few air-dwelling animals beside the bat are known to emit sound signals for the exclusive purpose of orientation in space.

---

[1] What is described here has sometimes been designated as "active" sonar. Inactive or "passive" sonar refers simply to underwater listening, without the emission of echo-ranging pulses.

Some nocturnal birds apparently do so (Griffin, 1953, 1958). Other animals, if crippled or injured by loss of sight, may develop some such method as a substitute for vision. A blind man, tapping with a cane, presents the closest human analogue to the echolocation of the bat. However, the avoidance of objects by the blind appears to be very crude when compared to the precise auditory perception of which bats are capable. Experimental observations suggest that blinded laboratory rats can find their way through a complicated apparatus by listening to the echoes from the sounds of their feet or from ultrasonic noises which they make (Anderson, 1954; Riley and Rosenzweig, 1957; Dashiell, 1959).

In the light of such knowledge, it would seem a reasonable inference that the method of orientation and navigation used by whales and porpoises must also be echolocation. The fact that vision is impractical in the sea and that other animals employ this method in the air both tend to support such an assumption. The idea that sonar is systematically used by the great whales and porpoises is, however, a new and intriguing thought. If true, it means that human beings did not invent navigation by sound in the ocean. The cetaceans probably evolved it and were using it for millions of years before the idea ever dawned upon man.

A hint of this possibility was given by McBride in 1947. Writing in his private notes at the Marine Studios of Marineland, Florida, where he was then curator, he reported that the bottlenose dolphin, when caught in a net, would roll or jump over a part of the net in which the cork floats had been pulled beneath the surface. This led him to suggest that the dolphin's "behavior calls to mind the sonic sending and receiving apparatus which enables the bat to avoid obstacles in the dark" (Schevill and McBride, 1956).

SOUNDS OF THE PORPOISE

In order to support such a theory, certain questions must be answered. One of the first of these questions concerns underwater noises made by whales and porpoises. Are these noises suitable for use as echo-ranging signals?

It is certainly true that the cetaceans are capable of producing many kinds of sounds. Observations of these noises, at least in the case of the dolphin, go back thousands of years and are in no sense modern discoveries. Thus, Aristotle wrote that the dolphin, "when taken out of water gives a squeak and moans in the air" (Thompson, 1910, iv. 9. 535*b*, 31). And Pliny the Elder, who certainly knew of Aristotle's statement, said, "for a voice they have a moan like a human being" (Rackham, 1947, ix. 23).

Of more recent interest is the statement by Kullenberg (1947) that, during a cruise on a Swedish research ship in the Mediterranean, dolphins, *Delphinus delphis,* at the bow of the ship gave off squeaks like "playing mice." Whistling dolphin sounds have also been reported by Fraser (1947) from a vessel off the coast of West Africa, and McBride (1940) has given an account of the noises made by porpoises, *Tursiops truncatus,* in an aquarium.

A phonograph recording of the sounds of captive porpoises was made by F. G. Wood, Jr., in 1952 (Wood, 1952, 1953). These noises have been variously described as "mewing," "rasping," "barking," and "whistling." The animals were kept in a large steel tank, however, in which there was some risk of reverberations or interfering noises. Recordings of porpoise sounds taken under less difficult conditions have been reported by W. Kellogg (1955) and by Kellogg, Kohler, and Morris (1953). These were made at Bimini and at the Daytona Sea Zoo. An analysis of the recorded noises has shown that the most common are (*a*) a bird-like or canary-like whistle, and (*b*) a rapid succession of clicking or clacking pulses, which occur in trains or series lasting several seconds or more. The underwater noises of the Mediterranean dolphin, *Delphinus delphis,* which have recently been analyzed by Vincent (1960), have also been found to contain whistles, "crackles," and mewings.

The whistle is undoubtedly what has been referred to by earlier writers as a "squeak." The rapid succession of sound pulses has been called "sputtering," "clicking," "rasping," "creaking," the "woodpecker sound," or the "rusty hinge sound." As to "mewing" and "barking," these, we think, are actually the same basic series of pulses, but in such instances they occur so rapidly that they take on a tonal quality of their own. If the clicks or pings within a train succeed one another slowly, they are heard by the listener as discrete and separate entities. When the rate of pinging is increased to around 20 per second, however, a tonal quality is introduced into the whole series because of the inability of the human brain to perceive such rates except as a homogeneous pattern. If now the pulses occur at several hundred a second, and the rate is varied within a single burst of pulses, the over-all effect may well be that of "moaning," "mewing," or "barking."

SOUNDS OF LARGER WHALES

That the larger whales are similarly capable of making noises in water has also been known for many years. Captain Sir William Parry, in his *Journal of a Voyage for the Discovery of the North West Passage from the Atlantic to the Pacific,* published in 1821, describes shrill sounds produced by the white whale, *Delphinapterus leucas.* When members of his crew got near, they heard the animals emit "a shrill ringing sound, not unlike that of musical glasses when badly played." The noises were heard best when the whales swam beneath the boat, "and ceased altogether on their coming to the surface" (p. 35). A century and a quarter later, the sounds of the same species were more clearly observed in the St. Lawrence Estuary by means of underwater listening gear. Schevill and Lawrence (1949) give interesting descriptions of the whistling and chattering of the *Delphinapterus* encountered at that time.

The noises of the pilot whale, *Globicephala macrorhyncha,* were described by Kritzler (1952), who had an excellent opportunity to study a specimen which lived in captivity for some time. He reported four kinds of sounds extending from a "loud smacking noise" to something like "the peevish whining of a young child." Even the sounds of the giant sperm whale have been heard through appropriate listening gear (Worthington and Schevill, 1957). They were picked up from the research vessel "Atlantis" off the coast of North Carolina. Subsequently, sperm whale noises were recorded by R. H. Backus from the vessel "Bear," 200 miles south of Cape Cod. Three types of noises were distinguished by the listeners. There can be no doubt from such observations that the dolphins as well as other toothed whales produce various sorts of sound waves in the ocean.

The whale-bone whales are also known to make noises in water. Describing a report published by the British Admiralty in 1946, Haan (1957, p. 20) observed that "the sounds of the fin whale under the surface of the sea resemble a flute tone from low to high, lasting about one second, and repeated at irregular intervals during about half a minute." A similar report was made by Schreiber (1952) in connection with SOFAR observations near the Hawaiian Islands. In this case, the hydrophone was at a depth of 2,100 feet. Sounds of a musical quality were picked up in the spring of the year during the mating season of two varieties of whales. Since they were definitely seasonal in occurrence and coincided with the presence of the whales, the noises were presumed to be made by these animals.

ECHO-RANGING SIGNALS

We have now to examine the question whether any of these sounds are the sorts of noises that might conceivably be used for echo-ranging or for navigation in the sea. The question at this point might be rephrased in the following way: Do any of the noises resemble the ranging or beaming signals of man's electronic sonar?

In the case of the dolphin, there is an obvious similarity—

which can be recognized merely by listening—between the rapid succession of pulses, or the "sputtering" sound, and the signals or pings sent out in mechanical sonar. The principal differences that can be distinguished at once are: (*a*) the frequency of emission of the porpoise pinging sound varies over a wide range, whereas that of human sonar is usually constant and (*b*) the intensity of the animal noises may also be markedly altered within a single burst of ranging signals.

The porpoise whistle, we think, could also be used in echo-ranging, although there is less likelihood of this. It would be what is known as a frequency-modulated signal. Since the pitch is continually changing, the returning echo at any instant would be different from the pitch of the tone being emitted at the source. The observations of its occurrence with captive animals, however, suggest that it is more likely to be some sort of a call. It may even have emotional significance. The situations in which it takes place and the behavior which accompanies it at times suggest that it is analogous to a cry of alarm. When a youngster is separated from its mother, a great deal of whistling ensues—particularly on the part of the baby. If an unusual or strange sound occurs, like that produced by playing water from a hose upon the surface of a porpoise enclosure, whistling usually results along with increased activity or "escape behavior" (W. Kellogg, 1959*a*).

The clicking or pinging sounds, on the other hand, fit well into the scheme of pulse-modulated sonar. A train of beaming signals made as the animal approaches a target would return a continuous series of echoes, each one occurring closer and closer to its original pulse. There would be a progressive reduction in the time interval between each echo and its signal. This would furnish a direct acoustical measure of distance.

Although the information with regard to whale sounds is not so well worked out, naturalistic observations again suggest that some of the noises are very much like porpoise sputterings. Thus, Schevill and Lawrence (1949) noted that the white whales which they heard emitted a great many "ticking and clicking" sounds. Kritzler (1952) observed that the noises of the pilot whale included a "peculiar grating snore similar to the sound much used by dolphins" (Kritzler, 1952, p. 328). As far back as 1840, Bennett wrote of the harpooned sperm whale, "When the whale descends to any considerable depth, a sound, which may be compared to the creaking of new leather, is conducted from its body along the line" (Bennett, 1840, p. 206). And the sperm whale noises recently described by Worthington and Schevill (1957) included underwater clicking. The occurrence of sonar-like noises made by whales would therefore seem to be well established.

WHALING WITH SOUND

Like fishermen, the whalers also have been alert to the commercial possibilities of making use of underwater sound transmission for the purpose of locating their catch. The usual sonar method can, of course, be employed for the distances within which sonar will operate. Ships with "active" sonar equipment can then attempt to find whales by bouncing echoes off their bodies.

Two other methods have also been proposed. The most obvious of these is the use of passive sonar—that is, the attempt to find whales by listening for the noises they emit. The principal difficulty with this procedure is that any whaling or large seagoing vessel, even with its engines stopped, is itself a source of considerable acoustical disturbance. Underwater ship noises are produced by pumps, blowers, fans, generators, and similar machinery. In a vessel of any size, it may be impossible to turn off the noisemaking equipment without losing control of the rudder, reducing steam pressure, or in other ways placing the ship in jeopardy. Under such conditions, any whale sounds which might occur would be masked or obscured by the interfering noises from the vessel itself.

Another method which has been suggested is to attempt to

53

control the direction of movement of whales or porpoises by luring them with underwater sounds. The Department of Fisheries of the Province of Newfoundland, Canada, has been interested in guiding pilot whales into coastal bays around Newfoundland by such a technique. This might consist of attracting or "calling" the whales by broadcasting their own recorded noises back into the water. Or, they might be enticed by the sounds of the organisms which they eat.

A contrasting, although related, method would be to frighten the animals into shallow water by loud or disturbing noises, as for example by underwater explosions. Gulf fishermen in the New Orleans area have investigated the possibility of using fear-inducing sounds to keep porpoises from taking fish from their nets and consequently from damaging the nets.

Chapter 5

The Nature
of the Signal

That porpoises and dolphins—and possibly other cetaceans as well—orient themselves in water by listening to the reflected echoes of their own noises is a notion that offers challenging possibilities for research. The opportunities for finding out new facts about this unique perceptual method are almost limitless, yet the field itself is a difficult one to examine. Special problems arise from the fact that man, the scientist, resides on land, while the subjects of his study exist in an alien medium. Much of the apparatus and equipment used must be placed under water, and some of it may actually have to be built under water. The research itself is, in fact, conducted in water, since the behavior to be observed occurs there. Problems arising from this situation do not enter into the study of echolocation in air-dwelling animals like the bat, for example.

In addition to such perplexities, one must consider the mere size and weight of a porpoise and the difficulties of maintaining even a single healthy specimen in captivity. Large numbers of experimental bats can be stored in a hibernating state in refrigerated containers. When used for research, they are simply removed and thawed out. A single porpoise, by contrast, must be fed as much as 18 pounds of fresh fish (or more) each day. It will eat nearly a ton of fish in three months. Moreover, the surroundings in which it lives and in which the research is conducted must be supplied with a continuous flow of salt water and must be kept clean and uncontaminated. These are some of the technical requirements of maintenance.

As to the demonstration of echolocation itself in these small whales, it seems to us that three sets of facts are necessary. First, it must be shown that the underwater noises emitted by porpoises fall within the temporal and frequency patterns suitable for echo-ranging in water. Second, it must be demonstrated that the senders of the noises can hear sufficiently well and possess sufficiently fine acoustic receptors to react to any echoes which are present. Third, it must be established—even though the animals may broadcast and receive appropriate auditory signals —that they actually use these signals as a means of navigating in the sea.

In the present chapter, we shall deal with the first of these problems. The others will be examined later. Here we shall look into the characteristics of the echo-ranging noises to find out what can be learned from analyzing them. Are any of the sounds ultrasonic? What is the nature of their echoes? How long do they last? Some information is available on these questions, although there is not nearly as much as we should like.

RECORDING AND LISTENING

The porpoise sounds which we have been able to analyze were picked up through various forms of hydrophones. Some of these were U.S. Navy AX 58's. Others were specially made. One hydrophone constructed for this work was capable of receiving vibrations up to and beyond 200,000 cycles per second

(200 kc.). It consisted of thick Rochelle salt blocks potted in clear plastic bonded to a brass cylinder containing a two-stage pre-amplifier. The signal from the pre-amplifier was fed into the input stage of a high-fidelity power amplifier. An underwater photograph of a hydrophone in use in porpoise research is reproduced in Plate III.

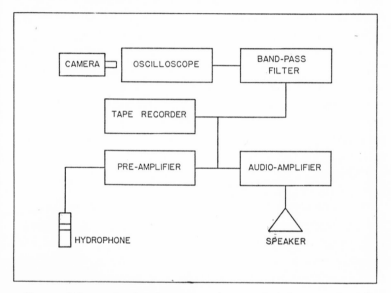

FIG. 2.—Scheme showing instrumentation required for recording the underwater sounds of the porpoise.

Many of the sounds, after being received in this manner, were then recorded by means of an Ampex model 307 high-speed tape recorder of the type ordinarily used in telemetering. The Ampex recorder has a rated recording range to 100,000 cycles per second (tape speed 60 inches per second), but will go considerably higher than this, although at reduced sensitivity. The response of the amplifier-recorder system as a whole was down approximately 3 decibels at 80,000 cycles per second, and 5 or 6 decibels at 100,000 cycles per second.

The noises from both captive and free-swimming porpoises were used in these observations. There were five captive animals. Two were young but mature females which were studied at the Lerner Marine Laboratory at Bimini. They were kept together in a wire enclosure, approximately 30 by 50 feet, through which sea water flowed freely. The third animal was confined alone in an excavated canal or pool about 40 by 60 feet, at the Daytona Sea Zoo at Daytona Beach. It was probably also a female. Two other captive specimens, one male and one female, were studied on many occasions at the Marine Laboratories of Florida State University, on the north coast of the Gulf of Mexico. Here they were maintained in an excavated enclosure whose sides and bottom were of soft marl or mud and were, therefore, essentially anechoic.

In addition to these, the sounds of numerous wild specimens were observed from a Navy launch which carried listening gear, recording equipment, and electronic filters. An unusual instance of small-boat recording was described in chapter 1.

ANALYZING THE NOISES

Three general methods were employed to determine the frequencies of the sounds which were emitted.

1. In the first of these methods, the porpoise noises, after being received by the hydrophone and amplified, were sent through band-pass or high-pass filters and observed on the screen of a cathode-ray oscilloscope (Morris, Kohler, and Kellogg, 1953). The arrangement of the apparatus is diagramed in Figure 2. One filter used in this work was an SKL variable electronic filter, model 302. The SKL filter is adjustable, permitting the passage of any desired frequency bands from zero to 200 kilocycles. When the lower frequencies were filtered out, the presence of the higher frequencies could be seen directly on the oscilloscope screen at the same time that the noises were being produced. A loud-speaker permitted the simultaneous hearing of the audible component of the sounds. Another filter,

employed particularly in studies of the wild porpoises in the Gulf, was a high-pass, high-Q filter which cut out all frequencies below 100 kilocycles.

2. The second method was a variation of the first, yet it afforded the opportunity for more careful and deliberate work. In this case, ultrasonic tape recordings obtained from the captive animals were played back on the Ampex recorder in the laboratory (see Plate V). The signals from the recorder were then sent through the SKL filter and were observed on an oscilloscope as in method (1). This procedure permitted repeated playbacks of the same sounds under favorable laboratory conditions, with the consequent opportunity of checking and rechecking the results obtained. A comparison of the same train of porpoise sound signals (*a*) photographed live and (*b*) from the playback tape is presented in Plate VI. The striking similarity between these cathode-ray pictures shows that the amount of distortion which is introduced by the playback method is very small indeed.

3. The third and most elaborate of the techniques for determining the frequencies within the total sound-complex made use of (*a*) a Panoramic Ultrasonic Analyzer, Model SB-7, and (*b*) a Fairchild Sound Measuring and Analyzing System.

a) The Panoramic Ultrasonic Analyzer is a scanning heterodyne receiver, which automatically measures the frequency and amplitude of both sonic and ultrasonic signals. By means of a stabilized sweeping system, ". . . the instrument tunes repetitively 6 times per second through a 200-kc. range in any part of a 10-kc. to 300-kc. band. As signals are tuned through, they appear on a cathode-ray tube as sharp vertical pips located horizontally in order of frequency. The heights of the pips indicate the relative magnitudes of their corresponding signals. A continuous overall graphic presentation of the spectrum is obtained on a long persistence cathode-ray tube screen." [1] The signals from the tape of the Ampex recorder were fed directly

[1] Statement from manufacturer.

into this device. A speaker was also in the circuit, so that the audible components of the sounds could be heard simultaneously with the occurrence of their pips upon the cathode-ray screen.

b) The Fairchild Sound Measuring and Analyzing System used in the frequency analysis is a special octave band-pass analyzing system manufactured by the Fairchild Instrument Company. The input signals are broken down into the octave bands by individual band-pass amplifiers having a maximum gain of 86 decibels. The filters are flat to ± 1.0 decibels over one-half of each octave band. At the cutoff points of the octave, the level is down 6 decibels from the center level, and the cutoff rate outside the octave band is 45 decibels per octave. The signals from Ampex tape recordings, after passing through the octave-band amplifiers of the Fairchild system, were read from a Dumont Model 304 oscilloscope and from a Ballentine AC meter, Model 310.

INTENSITY VERSUS FREQUENCY

The findings discussed here will deal only with the temporal and frequency characteristics of the noises made and will ignore any absolute measures of intensity. The reasons for this limitation are (*a*) that the receiving system as a whole was an uncalibrated system so far as intensities are concerned; yet (*b*), even had it been calibrated, there was no way to keep the distance between the porpoises and the hydrophone constant. Since the intensity of sound varies inversely with the square of the distance from the source, a receiving system calibrated for intensities would, therefore, have been of little value in any case.

Some hint as to absolute intensity of the clicks may be gained from the distance at which they can be heard with a hydrophone. On two occasions, we picked up the noises from porpoises estimated to be a half-mile away. The water depth in one case was 10 to 15 feet and in the other case from 15 to 25 feet. Although there was considerable wave noise, the signals came through clearly. It seems probable that, with deeper water, the ranging sounds of the animals would be transmitted several miles.

Even though our recording system was not calibrated for intensities, it was carefully checked for its frequency response. This was accomplished by sending pure tones from an oscillator through an underwater transducer, at from 20 to 200,000 cycles per second. The frequencies sent out by the transducer were then picked up by the hydrophone and amplifying equipment and were observed on the screen of an oscilloscope. The same frequencies were also sent directly to the oscilloscope, bypassing the underwater gear entirely. A comparison of the wave forms transmitted by these two methods showed that no distortions were introduced by the underwater system.

THE PORPOISE WHISTLE

The porpoise noises which occur most often are the whistle and the clicking sound. The whistle we found to be approximately 0.5 second in duration. It appeared in several melodies or pitch-patterns, the most common of which resembled the cheep of a canary. In our animals, this generally began in the neighborhood of 7,000 cycles per second and ended at about 15,000 cycles per second. The pitch-range was therefore slightly over an octave. Although harmonics are certainly present, we have not been able to bring them out well. The overtones which the whistle possesses are apparently weak and—so far as we can determine—do not extend beyond 20 kilocycles.

This is something of a paradox, since the whistle is, of course, very high to human ears and thus might be expected to possess a strong component of ultrasonic vibrations. However, since the whistle does occur in several forms, there may be varieties of it, not yet examined, which contain harmonics beyond 20 kilocycles. It is likely, moreover, that the whistles given by different individuals will vary considerably. A schematic representation, showing one form of the porpoise whistle—with frequency plotted against time—is given in Figure 3.

If the bottlenose dolphin employs the whistling sound to orient itself in space, this would constitute a kind of frequency-modulated sonar. The continuously changing pitch would reflect a continuously changing echo, which at any given instant

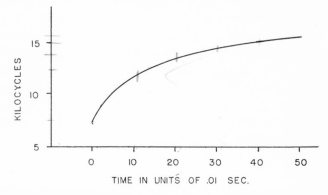

Fig. 3.—Schematic diagram of one form of the porpoise whistle, showing frequency plotted against time.

would differ from the frequency being produced. With such a method, it is not necessary that the sounds be emitted in short, intermittent bursts as they are in a pulse-modulated system.

UNDERWATER CLICKING

The second and by far the more common of the underwater sounds produced by the bottlenose dolphin is a series of rapid clicks or pings, sometimes described as the "rusty-hinge" sound, or the "creaking-door" sound. The rate at which the individual clicks occur may vary from as low as 5 per second to several hundred per second. In the latter instance, the total sound takes on the general quality of a groan or a bark. Within a single group of clicks lasting several seconds, the number of clicks per second can change from fast to slow, or vice versa. When these sounds occur at approximately 20 per second or slower, they lose any tonal quality that they may have possessed and are then heard as a succession of discrete individual units. In

62

such cases, each click becomes a sharp, staccato report—like that produced by striking a heavy wooden table with a small hammer.

Since the groan or barklike effect of a train of such clicks ordinarily is low in pitch, the average listener is not likely to suspect them of containing ultrasonic frequencies. Yet the methods of analysis previously described disclose them to be heavily weighted with such frequencies. The dominant vibrations, so far as acoustic energy is concerned, are in the sonic range, but other vibrations far above the limits of audibility are present. With respect to the wide band of frequencies represented, the clicks somewhat resemble white noise. Analysis of our Ampex recordings has shown a tapering-off of intensities from 20 to about 120 kilocycles, with the occasional occurrence of vibrations extending to 170 kilocycles or higher.

The tapering effect beyond 100 kilocycles undoubtedly is a function of the Ampex tape recorder, at least in part, since the performance of this instrument falls off rapidly above 100 kilocycles and is not even rated by the manufacturer for values higher than this level. At the same time, it may be due in some degree to the nature of the sounds themselves. So far as our observations go, it would appear that the different clicks in a series possess somewhere near the same complex of sonic and ultrasonic vibrations. But we are not too confident of this. If variations exist, they have not shown up in our procedures. It may be concluded, however, that trains or groups of porpoise sound pulses contain acoustic frequencies which extend to 120 kilocycles or above.

VIBRATIONS WITHIN A SINGLE CLICK

Does the frequency composition of the separate pulses vary from click to click? Are all sonar pings alike, or are there differences between them? So far as our present analysis goes, we can say that the combined frequencies within a train of clicks resemble white noise. But this need not mean that all the clicks are exactly the same, or even that the particular group of porpoise sounds which we have studied thus far is truly representative of all possible clicks. We do not know as yet whether the frequency composition within the clicks can vary. Nor do we know whether the acoustic frequency in the clicks is different from one train of clicks to another. We cannot know about *all* the clicks which are possible.

It is quite clear that a porpoise sometimes sends out a series of sonar-like pings at a very rapid rate. Under these conditions, one click follows another after an extremely short interval of time. On other occasions, the successive clicks in a series occur more slowly. Since a change of this kind—which can be easily observed—takes place so commonly, it is also possible that porpoises can alter the frequency composition of the individual pulses. Indeed, the auditory frequencies comprising any given sound pulse may be related to the rate at which the pulses in a train are emitted.

A variation in frequency composition from click to click might give the animal more information about the reflecting surface than if all the sounds were the same. It can be compared to taking a series of photographs of an object in different colored lights, or with different filters. The final answer to the question of frequency composition must await further, more precise, investigation. We can safely conclude now that there are many frequencies—both sonic and ultrasonic—in a train of clicks, although the individual clicks may not all be identical.

FREQUENCY SPECTRUM OF THE CLICKS

Plate VII (top) is a photograph of the cathode-ray screen of the ultrasonic analyzer, showing the frequency components occurring between 80 and 120 kilocycles in a series of these clicking sounds. All vibrations below 80 kilocycles have been filtered out, so that the record begins in the ultrasonic range at a point which is two full octaves above the upper limit of

64

human hearing (about 20 kilocycles). The 80-kilocycle marker-pulse is the low peak on the left which overlaps the higher peak on the left. Only those frequencies corresponding to the position of the sweep at the moment the sound occurred are shown. The separate peaks indicate the presence of frequencies within the different clicks, which correspond to the horizontal scale. The heights of the pips in the photograph give the relative intensities for the different frequencies.

The bottom picture in Plate VII shows another photograph which includes both the sonic and ultrasonic vibrations in a series of porpoise clicks. The tuning range of the analyzer in this instance was 0 to 200 kilocycles. The 200-kilocycle marker is the small pip on the extreme right. A marker showing 100 kilocycles appears as the heavier of the two central pips. It will be noted that there is a massing of frequencies below 25 kilocycles in this sample. At the same time, there are pips on the right representing vibration rates of 140, 155, and 170 kilocycles, respectively. Although these are the highest components which we have been able to photograph, there is no reason to believe that they represent the ultimate limit.

It is possible to derive an approximate frequency spectrum for the ultrasonic frequencies of these pinging sounds by noting the amplitudes of the pips on the screen of the ultrasonic analyzer for a large number of individual clicks. Such a frequency spectrum would indicate relative, rather than absolute, sound intensities, since these intensities are a function not only of the input signal but also of the recording system. The spectrum derived in this way for frequencies higher than 20,000 cycles per second is given in Figure 4.

A similar curve has also been obtained by a different method of analysis. In this case, Ampex recordings of dolphin sounds were run through a Fairchild Sound Measuring and Analyzing System. The graph obtained is essentially that reproduced in Figure 4.

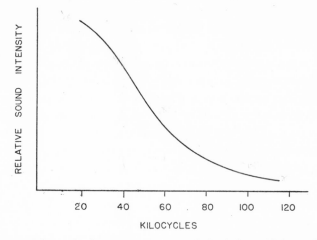

Fɪɢ. 4.—Ultrasonic frequency spectrum derived from high-speed tape recordings of the typical porpoise click. Essentially the same graph was obtained by two independent methods of acoustical analysis. (See Plate VII.)

CLICKS AS ECHO-RANGING SIGNALS

The clicks would be unsuitable for echo-ranging by a frequency-modulation method such as that applying to the whistle. On the other hand, a rapid succession of short pings would be excellent for echo-ranging, if time were allowed after each pulse for the reflecting back of its own echo. This, in fact, is the pulse-modulation method of echo-ranging.

So far as timing and duration are concerned, the clicks produced by the bottlenose dolphin fully satisfy the requirements necessary for echo-ranging in water by the pulse-modulation method. The duration of the shortest of these sounds has been found to be about 1 millisecond (0.001 second). Others are considerably longer. At a water temperature of 82.5° F. and a salinity approximately that of the water at Bimini, for example, sound in sea water travels 5,063 feet per second. In 0.001 second, it would, therefore, travel a distance of 5.06 feet. This means that the initial vibrations of a single click 0.001 second

66

in length would be reflected back to the point of emission at the termination of that click, from an object as close as 2.53 feet away. The speed with which a porpoise could react to this reflected signal would, of course, depend on additional factors, such as, for example, its reaction time. But, since the clicks are emitted in rapid succession, it is unlikely that the presence of any object would be sensed all at once. The approach to the object would be shown by a gradual change in the timing of the echo through many hundreds of successive impulses. An oscilloscopic picture of a train of porpoise clicks, each followed by its echo, is reproduced in Plate VIII.

ADVANTAGES OF MANY FREQUENCIES

The wide band of frequencies represented in these noises offers special advantages for echo-ranging in water because of the factors of masking and resolution.

1. Under ordinary circumstances, a porpoise may react to the sonic frequencies which it produces, but in many instances these frequencies would be masked or obscured by background water noise, which is mostly at lower frequency levels. Such noises as the sound of waves, the rushing of water past the animal's own body in fast swimming (like wind blowing past human ears), the sounds of ships' propellers, and the noises made by other organisms of the sea are generally most intense at frequencies below 10,000 cycles per second (Horton, 1959). When the basic porpoise frequencies are obscured or interfered with by such disturbances, the high-frequency components of the click would still filter through. It is possible that, in some cases, the ultrasonic vibrations alone would be all that could be heard.

An analogy to this situation in human experience would be an attempt to attract someone's attention in a large crowd—for example, in a hotel lobby or at a football game. A loud shout might not be heard at all, because it would be masked or muffled by the interfering hubbub of so many other voices. But a sound of higher pitch, like whistling, would penetrate the vocal clatter.

2. High frequencies would also be better for the inspection of an object by sound, because they are shorter in wave length and have a greater resolving power or directionality. They would consequently indicate the size and shape of a nearby target, by echoes, better than long waves. A tone of 5,000 cycles per second, for example, if transmitted at a sound speed of 5,000 feet per second, produces a wave 1.0 foot in length. But, if the frequency is increased to 50,000 cycles per second, the sound speed remaining the same, the wave length becomes 0.1 of a foot. The higher the vibration rate, the shorter the wave length and therefore the more precise the resolution, as determined from the reflected echo.

3. There is also the phenomenon that low sonic frequencies travel greater distances than high frequencies, since the high frequencies attenuate more. In this respect the different wave lengths complement each other. The higher frequencies, as we have seen, would be beneficial at close range for detailed examination of an object whose presence had already been determined. But the low frequencies—if masking noise was absent—could be used to detect more distant objects which could not be discovered by ultrasonic waves. This means that the low-frequency components of a porpoise sound-ping would be useful for a rough general orientation in the environment.

It is even possible that this varying property of the different frequencies would serve as a cue to the distance of a reflecting target. A faraway object, not reached by ultrasonic vibrations, could be "tuned in" from the same transmitting point by the lower frequencies. The precise vibration rate at which its echoes were received would serve as an additional measure of its distance —quite beyond the latency or intensity of the returning echo.

SEEING AND HEARING ECHOES

The echoes which are produced by porpoise clicks can be clearly demonstrated in at least two ways.

1. They can be seen and photographed on the screen of a cathode-ray oscilloscope. A train of clicks, each followed by its echo, is shown in the oscilloscopic photograph reproduced in Plate VIII. It will be noticed from this picture that the intensity of the echoes, as indicated by the changing size of the secondary spikes to the right of each click, varies with time according to a different sequence than does the intensity of the clicks. This is because of the changing position of the porpoise (or the source of the clicks) with respect to the hydrophone and the reflecting target.

2. Porpoise echoes can also be *heard* by the human ear under the proper acoustical and temporal conditions. The actual hearing of the echoes which occur is accomplished by reducing the play-back speed of the recording tape. This brings the entire auditory pattern within the more limited perceptual range of the human ear and brain.

The original tape speed of the Ampex ultrasonic recorder is 60 inches per second. Tests have been made with play-back speeds of 1/8, 1/16, 1/32, and 1/64 of the recording rate. This has the effect of lowering the intensity as well as the number of cycles per second of the sounds which are played. For example, a bona fide frequency of 100,000 cycles per second, reproduced at 1/64 of its original speed, becomes 1,562.5 cycles per second. The duration of the sound is correspondingly lengthened by a factor of 64. Under such circumstances, the echo becomes clearly audible. It can be heard by most people at 1/16 of the recording speed, is very clear at 1/32, and is often a booming reverberation at 1/64 of the original rate.

An inherent difficulty in measuring the duration of any single click is brought to light by this slow play-back method, since a click cannot often be clearly separated from its own echo. One would have to be certain, in obtaining precise time measurements of this sort, that there was no echo at all—a difficult, if not impossible, requirement.

69

HOW ARE THE SOUNDS MADE?

The question of just how the dolphin produces sound signals has not yet been completely explained. The cetaceans, like the fishes, possess no vocal cords (Haan, 1957, p. 20). As far back as 1901, Benham (1901, p. 295) wrote on this subject: "Two points of general interest are presented by the larynx of the Cetacea: firstly, the absence of the vocal cords, and even any rudiment of them; secondly, the peculiar modifications undergone in the arytenoid cartilege."

Since "vocalization" is eliminated as the source of the ranging signals, what one thinks of next is the powerful valve of the blowhole. This can be vibrated like a human lip when air is blown past it. Captive porpoises have, in fact, been trained to "sing" in the air by apparently doing just this. On command they will stand on their tails and emit a noise from the exposed blowhole which is reminiscent of a Bronx cheer. If the vibration rate is raised to a sufficiently high level, the resulting effect is somewhat like the human voice. If, on the other hand, the individual pulses making up the sound are slowed down, they become clearly identifiable as porpoise clicks or pings. When one hears these noises made in the air from a distance of a few feet, there can be no doubt that they are the same as the basic sonar signal with which we are familiar.

Are they produced by the vibrating lip of the blowhole itself? We have not yet been able to convince ourselves that this is so. When trained dolphins emit the clicking sound in the air, the blowhole appears to remain open. The noises seem definitely to be coming from or *through* the half-opened orifice, just as a note which is sung can pass through the lips of a singer. This does not necessarily mean that such sounds are *caused* by the lips, or that they are made *at* the lips. Some other vibrating mechanism below the porpoise blowhole could conceivably produce the noises.

If the sound is caused by the passage of air, and if the air is expelled from the blowhole as it is made, one should be able to see a stream of bubbles when the noises are emitted under water. Fraser (1947) reported that he saw such bubbles coming from the blowholes of dolphins swimming at the bow of a ship in the English Channel. He heard no sounds, although he thought the animals might be making them. Tomilin (1947*a*), who observed captive specimens of the common dolphin, *Delphinus delphus,* in the Black Sea, also declares that bubbles did emerge as the animals emitted noises.

Unfortunately, we have not been able to confirm these findings in the case of the bottlenose porpoise. In the Bahama Islands, where the water is extremely clear, skin divers went beneath the surface to study captive dolphins. To eliminate any doubt about the occurrence of the noises, a hydrophone picked them up, they were properly amplified at the dockside next to the enclosure, and were then sent back to the observer who listened through waterproof earphones. On no occasion when the sounds were being made were we ever able to detect a telltale stream of bubbles.

The problem was subsequently approached by an entirely different method. Compressed air was blown upward through the blowhole of a dead porpoise head after it had been severed. By manipulating the external valve as the air passed through, it was possible, it is true, to produce a few feeble noises. But the demonstration was far from convincing, and the sounds which occurred had little resemblance to real porpoise clicks. Of course, a flaccid blowhole is hardly the same as a live one with internal power furnished by active muscles.

SOUNDS FROM BENEATH THE BLOWHOLE

Are the noises made by some vibrating part located inside of the blowhole, but below its external valve? Such a vibrating mechanism apparently exists. The nasal passage underneath the blowhole contains a number of diverticula or air pockets. Just below the surface orifice, these expand laterally on either side of the central canal. Farther down there is an anterior pocket as the single opening divides into the nares at the level of the skull. There are also tongue-like projections within the air passage which probably act as secondary valves during submersion. "The overlapping and close-fitting-together of the lips and walls of the passage form a series of check valves . . ." (Lawrence and Schevill, 1956, p. 147). One or more of these could conceivably vibrate or clack either by muscular action or by a rapid flow of

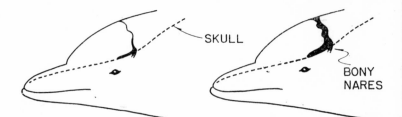

Fig. 5.—Diagram showing probable action of the blowhole in closed (*left*) and open (*right*) positions. The external valve and the anterior-posterior projecting processes are indicated. Auditory vibrations could conceivably be made either by the lip of the blowhole, or lower down in the passage (modified from Howell).

air. Even if the external blowhole were closed, the inner structures might well be free to operate. The general arrangement of some of these parts (excluding the lateral air cavities) is diagramed in Figure 5. This, we are inclined to believe, is the most likely source of the dolphin's noises.[2]

Some support for an explanation of this sort is furnished by the observations of Dr. Kenneth Norris of the University of California at Los Angeles. Working with a blindfolded porpoise at the Pacific Oceanarium at Palos Verdes, California, he discovered that the animal had difficulty in locating a target like a fish when it was presented below the level of the porpoise's face or mouth. No such difficulty existed if the target was on a line

[2] An excellent and detailed anatomical study of the blowhole has been made by Lawrence and Schevill (1956).

with the mouth or above the mouth. This would indicate at least that the clicks come out of, or from a place near, the top of the head. Even assuming the sounds are not highly directional, a target which is screened from the source of the sounds by the animal's own body would furnish poor or garbled echoes.

Chapter 6

The Acoustic Analyzer

Although the sonar click of the porpoise contains ultrasonic vibrations, this is not an exclusive characteristic of porpoise noises alone. Other animals also make sounds extending well beyond the upper limit of human hearing. Thus, Anderson (1954) has shown that the noises of some rodents, of marmosets, and of squirrel monkeys have ultrasonic frequencies. We also know that bats (Griffin, 1958) and certain insects (Pierce, 1948) emit similar high-frequency sound waves.

The percussive or staccato nature of the porpoise click makes its ultrasonic components less difficult to understand, perhaps, than the tonal ultrasonics of some other organisms. Many impact or colliding noises, like those occurring when one hard object strikes another, contain frequencies covering a wide band—including ultrasonics. An example of such a sound is the explosive ringing produced when a heavy hammer strikes an anvil. In view of the natural composition of such inanimate noises, one might suspect the clicks of the porpoise to be constituted in a similar fashion.

The questions to be dealt with now concern the function of these ultrasonic frequencies and whether a porpoise can respond to them. This, it will be recalled, is the second of the steps set down in chapter 5 as necessary to demonstrate the process of echo-ranging. The sound signals have been shown to be particularly well suited to serve as sonar pulses. Is the acoustic organ which these animals possess capable of dealing with such signals? What of the range and sensitivity of the ear? How is the receptor affected by the pressure of deep water? Although we cannot answer these questions conclusively, we can at least get a probable answer to them.

THE STRUCTURE OF THE RECEPTOR

Even a superficial examination of the ears of the cetaceans suggests that they are capable of extraordinary hearing. The ears of the *Odontoceti,* of which the bottlenose dolphin is a member, are far more sensitive from the standpoint of structure than the ears of other whales (Yamada, 1953). They have "attained a degree of development practically unknown in the animal kingdom," writes Haan (1957, p. 21). There is no external pinna, and the meatus of the outer ear is so small that it is difficult to find. This tiny canal may remain entirely closed during dives, but even if this is so, it should not affect the functioning of the auditory mechanism. The pressure waves of the water would be transmitted through the body tissues directly to the middle ear. Haan (1957, pp. 51–53) experimentally demonstrated this fact, using a piece of whale blubber. One view is that the meatus and surrounding muscles perform the functions of a depth or pressure gauge (Yamada, 1953, p. 4), which would be a necessary organ for these diving mammals.

Perhaps the most striking aspect of the receptor is that the middle and inner ears are together in a single osseous complex known as the tympano-periotic bone or bones. They are not imbedded in the skull, as is the case with other mammals. By contrast, these bony parts are set out from the cranium as appendages and are attached to it only by ligaments. The tympanic and periotic bones are of extremely hard substance—like the enamel on teeth—which can be sawed or cut only with difficulty. According to one student of this subject, they are the hardest bones known in any animal. As a consequence, they do not disintegrate with time like the other bones of the skeleton. Such "ear bones," known as "cetoliths," are occasionally dredged from the floor of the ocean.

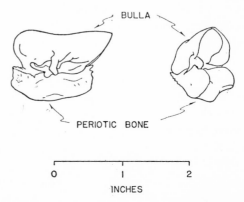

BULLA

PERIOTIC BONE

0   1   2

INCHES

Fig. 6.—Side and end views of the tympanic bulla and the periotic bones of the porpoise ear. The ossicles (not shown here) lie between these two bony parts. The cochlea and vestibular canals are in the periotic bone.

The periotic bone contains the vestibule, the cochlea, and the semicircular canals. The tympanic bulla which adjoins it is a curved, shell-like structure which is fastened to the periotic bone on one side. Just how these parts function is by no means clear, and different views are held by different authorities (Fraser and Purves, 1954, 1960; Haan, 1957, 1960; R. Kellogg, 1928; Yamada, 1953). One explanation is that the modified tympanum, although present, no longer receives vibrations, but that the transmission of sounds from the water to the cochlea is by bone conduction. Another theory is that the bulla is set into vibration by resonance and that its movement is transmitted to the inner ear by the ossicles which lie between it and the periotic bone. A third interpretation is that the ear responds essentially like the ear of a terrestrial animal, and that the water vibrations are translated into air vibrations, which then act upon the tympanum. The complex sinus system which these animals possess is undoubtedly associated with the reception of auditory stimuli.

The cochlea of all of the *Odontoceti* is enlarged compared with the vestibular canals. It rotates from 1¾ to 2 turns. A unique aspect of the cochlear structure is described by Yamada and Yoshizaki (1959, p. 303). We learn from these authors that "the secondary lamina spiralis develops up to as far as 68–82% of the cochlear canal. There is evidence that the slit between this and the primary lamina spiralis coincides, within this range, with the actual basilar membrane. In the first 50% range, the basilar membrane increases its width at an extremely slow rate, generally between 0.1–0.2 mm. This is probably related to the high frequency hearing capability of those animals."

OTIC ADAPTATIONS TO PRESSURE

The dissection of fresh specimens has shown that the space between the bulla and the periotic bone is filled with air or "foam." This means that there are media of different compressibility on opposite sides of it. Vibratory waves of water (or of animal tissue) on its outer surface could conceivably cause it to move without much interference, since the inner surface is not damped by a substance of equal resistance. An arrangement of this sort would be much more favorable for the accurate transmission of rapid oscillations than is the case in air-dwelling mammals whose tympanic membrane has material of the same kind on each side.

The reason why the tympano-periotic unit is independent from and can move in relation to the skull is, no doubt, to take care of differences in pressure due to water depth. In a sense, the ear "floats" with reference to the skull. It can move in or out as the external pressure of the water changes, without having one of its units (the tympanic bulla) displaced with respect to the other (the periotic bone). If these ear parts had been hollowed out of the bones of the cranium, an increase in the external pressure would disturb their operation—just as pressure changes on one side of the human tympanum interfere with its freedom of motion. An ear which is completely external to the skull can "give" as the pressure increases; it can adjust in some degree to external conditions.

From anatomical features such as these, it is evident that the acoustic receptor of the bottlenose dolphin has undergone a remarkable adaptation in the course of geologic time. The result is a marvellously sensitive organ, especially adjusted for the reception of vibratory pressure waves in water.

THE EIGHTH NERVE

No organism can react to auditory stimuli with its ears alone. The auditory or eighth cranial nerve, the intermediate ganglia, and the projection centers of the brain must also take part in the process. It was a custom of I. P. Pavlov (1927, p. 110), the great Russian physiologist, to include all the units which function in any receptor system under the general heading "analyzer." Hence, the ear, its neural connections, and the appropriate brain centers would be called "the acoustic analyzer." Let us turn then to the neural aspects of this analyzer.

The acoustic nerve is considerably larger than the optic nerve in the porpoise; but it is the cochlear, rather than the vestibular, branch which has reached this unusual stage of development. The nerve itself does not appear to contain an excessive number of fibers. What contributes to its size is the very large diameter of many of these. This may mean a more rapid transmission of nerve impulses and, consequently, the transmission of a greater number of impulses per second than is the case with smaller fibers.

The acoustic geniculate is also very large, as are the other auditory nuclei and tracts within the brain stem. In most mammals, the optic colliculus exceeds the size of the acoustic colliculus by far. But the opposite is true for the porpoise. Here, the optic colliculus is not more than one-fourth as large as the acoustic (R. Kellogg, 1928, p. 204). All of this points to the special significance of the sense of hearing in the bottlenose dolphin.

PORPOISE HEMISPHERES

The proportions of the brain and cerebral hemispheres further substantiate this observation. Its size in relation to the human brain has already been discussed (see chap. 2). The hemispheres are tremendous, and the cerebral cortex contains an unusual number of convolutions and sulci. Three separate papers by Langworthy (1931*a*, 1931*b*, 1932) have dealt with the central nervous system of the porpoise. Langworthy found the cerebral hemispheres to be more highly differentiated with respect to convolutions than the cerebral hemispheres of man (1932, p. 485). More recently, the porpoise brain has been described by Lilly as having "a complexity as great, if not greater, than that of the human" (Brazier, 1959, p. 108). Kruger (1959, p. 175) regards the dolphin and the human brain as strikingly similar in "the extensive development of the cerebral cortex, the cerebellum and of the ventral portion of the pons."

The most extraordinary feature of the brain as a whole is the fact that it is considerably wider than it is long. Its lateral diameter, in other words, exceeds its anterior-posterior diameter. This is in striking opposition to the general design of the brains of other animals and of human beings. The customary cerebral pattern set down by nature is for the hemispheres to be longer than they are wide. The reversed proportions of the dolphin brain again would suggest a kind of supersensitivity for the analysis of sound. This follows from the fact that the sensory pathways beginning in the eighth nerve terminate in the auditory projection areas on the lateral surface of each hemisphere. "On the basis of these acoustic impulses, the temporal lobe has greatly increased in size," says Langworthy (1931*b*, p. 234).

This remarkable development in the temporal region parallels the enlargement of the frontal lobes in man, or the unusual size

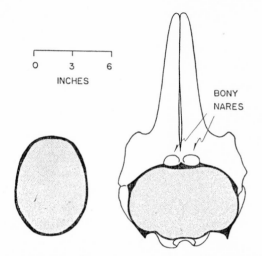

Fig. 7.—A comparison of the brain cavity of a porpoise with that of an adult human being. The tops of the skulls were sawed off for these diagrams. The human skull is on the left. The frontal portion of both skulls points upward. The lateral dimension of the porpoise brain is greater than its anterior-posterior dimension. This is reversed from the proportions of the human brain and that of other mammals.

of the olfactory bulbs in the dog. Just as the keen sense of smell in the dog is reflected in the size of its olfactory centers, so the anatomy of the porpoise brain implies an exceptional ability for the analysis of auditory stimuli. The porpoise cerebrum has a kind of superacoustic development which in turn suggests a capacity with regard to sound perception that may far exceed that of other animals. One supposes that the decoding and analysis of fine gradations of sound signals is facilitated by

80

a greater number of cortical neurones taking part in the final process.

Breathnach (1960) has recently reviewed more than 150 references dealing particularly with the central nervous system of the cetaceans. With regard to audition, he writes (p. 224), "The importance of auditory impressions to the economy of Cetacea appears to be directly associated with the large size of the cochlear nerve and the relatively enormous development of the auditory end-stations." The evidence is clearer, perhaps, in the case of the bottlenose dolphin, than with many of the other cetaceans. All of the body parts concerned with audition are modified or accelerated in their development. The bottlenose dolphin would seem, in fact, to be literally "built for sound." The *Odontoceti,* and particularly the porpoises and dolphins, may well possess the finest acoustic analyzer of any animal, including even the bats.

Also of importance is the surprising fact that the sense of smell is completely lacking in the dolphin and the olfactory lobes and olfactory tracts are missing altogether (Haan, 1957, p. 20; Kruger, 1959, p. 177). This is in contrast to the situation with fishes, whose olfactory lobes are large and functional. The olfactory sense, in a way, is "slower" than the sense of hearing and is less accurate for distance perception. Is it possible that, in the bottlenose dolphin, the acoustic analyzer has taken over whatever service the sense of smell might once have been able to contribute?

THE LIVING BRAIN

Attempts to study the actual functioning of the brain by exposing and mapping the cortical areas of living porpoises have thus far proved futile. The fundamental difficulty thwarting such work is that the porpoise seems to be incapable of being anesthetized for surgical study. Whenever a general anesthetic is given, even in carefully controlled doses, the animal stops breathing and dies (Lilly, 1958). The technical solution to the difficulty is probably to employ artificial respiration.

What all this means, however, is that the centers controlling respiration probably lie in the cerebral cortex rather than in the brain stem, as is the case with man and other mammals. The so-called breathing center may be in the motor area of the cerebral cortex which, like the temporal lobes, is also large and well developed. If this is true, it follows that respiration in the bottlenose dolphin is a conscious or voluntary activity rather than automatic or involuntary. Anesthetizing drugs which primarily affect the cortex but not the lower centers will not work in such instances. By stopping the voluntary cortical processes, they interfere with breathing and produce death by suffocation.

It seems quite logical that an air-breathing mammal which lives in the sea must always be consciously aware of exactly where it is before it ever takes a breath. Otherwise, it might accidentally inspire while submerged—and so drown itself. The situation is quite different with man, who—no matter where he is or whether conscious or unconscious—always resides in a life-sustaining environment of air. Again, we have evidence of the special adaptation and unusual development of the cerebral cortex in the bottlenose dolphin.

OBSERVATIONS OF HEARING AT SEA

Since the structure of the acoustic analyzer points so strongly to a kind of super hearing, there should exist behavioral descriptions to support such an inference. And this, indeed, is the case. As far back as the ancient Greeks, it seems to have been suspected that dolphins have a keen sense of hearing. According to the Greek poet Pindar (522–443 B.C.), they could be lured to the surface of the water by the sounds of the lyre and the flute (Haan, 1957). In order that they might save him in a time of crisis, Arion is supposed to have called dolphins to his ship by singing and by playing on a cithara (Godley, 1920, I, 24). In our time, it has been observed on numerous occasions that porpoises will disappear in haste from a vessel at the sound of a supersonic echo-sounder (Howell, 1930, p. 73; Fraser, 1947). The shot from a .22-caliber rifle "will make all porpoises within a mile or so swim rapidly seaward" (McBride and Hebb, 1948, p. 112). Such behavior is quite different from the stolid unresponsiveness of the fishes to water-borne noises (Moulton and Backus, 1955; see also chap. 3).

It is highly probable that the larger whales are also very sensitive to auditory stimuli, but present information on this subject is much more meager. On a voyage southward across the Gulf of Mexico in July, 1953, a lookout on the Coast Guard cutter "Tampa" sighted a group of approximately twenty sperm whales. The position of the ship was then at latitude 26° 04′ N. and longitude 89° 22′ W., or about 200 miles from the nearest land. The vessel reduced speed and proceeded slowly in the direction of the swimming animals. At a distance of about a mile, a giant member of the herd—estimated to be 60 feet in length—was seen to make a tremendous leap from the water at an angle of approximately 45 degrees. At the peak of its trajectory, the head and eyes of the animal must have been 30 feet or more above the surface. It then fell back amid a great geyser of spray.

This incident was interpreted on shipboard as a reaction to the underwater sounds from the propeller and engines of the "Tampa." These mechanical water-borne noises must have been audible to the whales for a considerable time before they were sighted. The whale which left the water—because of its great size—was judged to be a bull. Probably it was the leader of the herd. The object of the enormous leap, it was thought, was to investigate the strange noises by vision and to discover the distance and nature of the source of the sounds.

Examples such as this are interesting, even exciting. But, their interpretation leans so heavily on inference that not much can be concluded from them.

CONDITIONING TESTS OF HEARING

What are needed are some experimental measurements of the sensitivity of the ear. Tests of this sort have, in fact, been attempted by Schevill and Lawrence (1953*a*, 1953*b*, 1954). They were conducted with a single captive porpoise in a tidal inlet at Marineland, Florida.

By means of the conditioned-reflex method, these investigators broadcast pure tones of various frequencies into the water. The reinforcing or unconditioned stimulus on any given trial was a food-fish, which was immersed after the conditioned tonal signal had been given. The experimenters reported that the porpoise came for the food on less than 50 per cent of the trials when the conditioned stimulus was higher than 126,000 cycles per second (126 kc.). It seemed to come on more than 50 per cent of the trials for frequencies lower than 126 kilocycles. As a consequence, they concluded that the upper threshold of hearing for the porpoise being tested was 126,000 cycles per second. This figure is far higher than the upper frequency threshold reported for any other animal.

The fundamental assumption behind such a conclusion is that the only way the animal could tell when a fish was available was by means of the tonal signal given by the experimenters. If the porpoise approached the feeding station after the signal had been made, its approaching behavior was regarded as a response to the tone. If it failed to approach, it was presumed not to have heard the tone. Unaccounted for in such reasoning is the fact that the porpoise was undoubtedly able to find the fish by itself—without any tonal signal whatever. Information now available shows that a bottlenose dolphin can detect the presence of a fish—or any other object in the water—by means of its own echo-ranging system. Under these circumstances, the precise role which the conditioning tones played in the fish-taking behavior becomes highly problematical. At least, the

results regarding high-frequency hearing are of doubtful or uncertain validity.

USE OF THE AVOIDANCE METHOD

Another quite different procedure, not subject to this criti-
cism, was employed in studies of ultrasonic hearing by the present writer and associates (W. Kellogg and Kohler, 1952; W.
Kellogg, 1953). The measurements in this instance made use
of the avoidance, rather than the approaching, principle. Thirteen bottlenose porpoises were used in the research. They were
tested at three separate places, two of which were in Florida and
one in the Bahama Islands.

Ten of the animals were observed at the Marine Studios at
Marineland, Florida, where they were kept together in a circular steel tank 14 feet deep and 75 feet in diameter. The water
was filtered, permitting visibility through windows in the walls
of the tank below the surface for the full diameter of 75 feet.
All observations at Marineland were made through these windows below the water line.

Two further specimens were examined at the Lerner Marine
Laboratory at Bimini. Here they were kept together in an off-
shore wire enclosure about 30 by 50 feet. The depth of the water
in the Bimini enclosure was about 7 feet at low tide and 10 feet
at high tide. The bottom was of white coral sand, and the water
was naturally clear. Observers stood above the surface upon a
pier or dock at the edge of the enclosure.

The thirteenth animal was a trained specimen, which had
been in captivity for about two years. It was examined alone in
an excavated pen or pool at the Daytona Sea Zoo. The pen was
a part of a long canal about 40 feet wide and 8 to 10 feet deep,
into which tidal water flowed. Both ends of the pen, which was
about 60 feet long, were of wire fencing, and the bottom was
soft sand, with some mud. Although fairly free from sediment,
the water was a clear brown color, with visibility not exceeding

1 or 2 feet. The dolphin could therefore not be seen when it was submerged. Nevertheless, the observations of this animal were in some ways more significant than any of the others, since they afforded the opportunity for studying a single individual in isolation, uninfluenced by the activity of other organisms.

The ages of the two dolphins at the Bimini laboratory were estimated to be about four years. Both of them were females. Most of the animals at Marineland (including both sexes) were older, as judged by their size and weight. The age of the Daytona specimen was unknown, although it was mature. It was probably also a female.

SOUND-TRANSMITTING GEAR

The sound-producing gear consisted of a Hewlett-Packard Model 200C oscillator, capable of transmitting sine waves of from 20 to 200,000 cycles per second. The signal of the oscillator was fed through a 20-watt amplifier whose output was essentially linear to 100,000 cycles per second into a USRL-type 1K underwater speaker or transducer loaned by the United States Navy on ONR contract. The transducer was capable of emitting frequencies at least to 200,000 cycles per second (200 kc.), although at reduced and variable intensities beyond 10,000 cycles per second (10 kc.). The system as a whole was consequently uncalibrated for intensities. Since the object was not to measure intensity thresholds, the power output of the amplifier was simply increased for the higher vibration rates.

However, the accurate transmission of the different frequencies, even though at varying intensities, was carefully checked in underwater sound tests, by the use of a special hydrophone and sound pick-up apparatus, which recorded through an oscilloscope. The signal for a given frequency would first be sent directly to the cathode-ray tube of the oscilloscope, bypassing the underwater gear entirely. The same signal would then be projected and picked up under water and again observed on the tube of the oscilloscope. A comparison of the direct and underwater signals on the screen of the cathode-ray tube showed that the wave form was transmitted through water without distortion for the entire frequency range up to 200 kilocycles.

THE TECHNIQUE OF TESTING

In the tests themselves, the animals were stimulated by pure tones, in short bursts or beeps 1 to 3 seconds in duration, sent through the water by means of the transducer. The frequencies of these tones were randomly varied between 100 and 200,000 cycles per second. Clicks and other on-and-off artifacts were avoided by the elimination of make-and-break switches. Each stimulus was begun and ended by a volume control and so had a gradual onset and termination. The interval between successive stimuli extended from 30 seconds to several minutes in length. The development of adaptation to repeated sound stimuli was discouraged and retarded by interspersing the different sessions with long rest periods and by limiting the length of each session. From two to four observers were constantly watching the animals whenever any sound tests were made. An underwater photograph of a porpoise swimming near a model of the 1K transducer is shown in Plate IV.

Whether a particular stimulus was "heard" or reacted to was at once apparent from the nature of the swimming behavior which occurred. Porpoises will avoid unusual sounds (Howell, 1930, p. 73; Fraser, 1947; McBride and Hebb, 1948, p. 112). In most instances, the reaction to a strange noise appears to be a kind of startle or flight reaction. The speed and rhythm of the swimming movements made by the trunk and tail flukes increase abruptly, and an entirely different "gait" or rate of locomotion is immediately assumed. If swimming space permits, captive porpoises will usually (although not always) dash rapidly away from the source of the sound. If there is no opportunity for avoidance or escape, they will suddenly swim faster in the original or in some different direction—in a kind of disturbed or "emotional" response pattern. The change in behavior is perfectly obvious and is not at all difficult to see. What is taking place is clear even to the uninitiated.

TESTS AT MARINELAND

To use this avoidance behavior as an indication of acoustic sensitivity, the swimming before and after each beep or burst of sound was directly compared. In the first series of tests conducted at Marineland, accelerated swimming responses of this sort were consistently and uniformly produced by all frequencies between 100 cycles per second and 50,000 cycles per second. Considerable attention was given to the higher frequencies, and there can be little question about this finding. Since responses occurred regularly to the 50-kilocycle stimulus, this figure, if taken as a threshold reading, should be regarded as the highest, 100 per cent, point. Frequencies higher than this were not consistently reacted to. No attempt was made to explore the lower threshold for pitch, and no sounds below 100 cycles per second were transmitted.

It was noted in the first observations at Marineland that the speed-up in swimming was not easy to obtain between 100 and 400 cycles per second. In order to get a reaction within this frequency range, it was necessary to raise the gain or output of the apparatus by a considerable amount. When the intensity was increased in this way and responses occurred, the nature of these reactions for frequencies between 100 and 400 cycles per second was often more violent and disturbed than that produced by the other frequencies. The animals sometimes dived out of the water, and occasionally made swerving "attacks" or "charges" in the direction of the transducer, instead of swimming away from it. A human evaluation of such behavior might characterize it as "anger" rather than "fear."

This result was obtained only in the circular tank at Marineland and never in the later determinations at Bimini or at Daytona. The effect is to be attributed, we think, to the high level of background water noise existing in the steel tank at Marineland—a noise level which was itself of low frequency. An increase in the energy of the low-frequency stimuli which was intense enough to break through this interference may also have stimulated the tactual receptors of the animals with pressure waves. In such cases, they would have "felt" the vibrations on the skin (W. Kellogg and Kohler, 1952). At any rate, this phenomenon was entirely absent in the quiet water at the Lerner Laboratory and at Daytona Beach, and at these places no qualitative difference was observed in the nature of the responses to any stimulus, no matter what its vibration rate.

TESTS AT BIMINI

In the second series of tests on the two young animals at the Lerner Laboratory, the usual flight responses occurred regularly to vibrations as high as 80,000 cycles per second (80 kc.). These results were again carefully checked and rechecked, and we are confident that there can be no error in this approximate threshold level. The figure of 80 kilocycles is again a 100 per cent value, not a 50 or 75 per cent threshold point.

The difference between the two results of 50,000 and 80,000 cycles per second may in part be due to the youthfulness of the porpoises at Bimini, since the upper limit of hearing is known to decrease in many organisms with age. Perhaps a more satisfactory interpretation, and the one which now seems to us to be the correct one, would explain the discrepancy in terms of the varying conditions under which the two sets of tests were conducted. The difference again is traceable, we think, to the high noise level in the steel tank at Marineland. Sounds of the pumping of water, of drainage, of water currents, and of splashing were continuous. At Bimini, on the other hand, since tidal water flowed freely through the wire fencing of the outdoor enclosure, no pumping or drainage was necessary. As a result, the noise level of the water was much lower. Quite likely, therefore, it was the interference caused by uncontrolled water noise which produced the lower reading in the first instance.

TESTS AT DAYTONA BEACH

A final check made with the isolated dolphin which was tested at Daytona generally confirmed the earlier findings. Since the Daytona animal had been in captivity a long time, it spent a good deal of time floating (without swimming) at the top of the water—ogling the human beings on land first with one eye and then the other. But as soon as the transducer had been lowered into the water, the porpoise submerged and began a slow and deliberate swimming about the enclosure, mostly at the end farthest from the instrument. Because of the opacity of the water, the location of the animal could not always be determined, except when it came up for air.

Such conditions did not at first appear to favor the observation of any behavior changes. Yet it soon became apparent that whenever a sound was projected into the water, the position of the animal, its speed, and its direction of motion could be determined. These were indicated by the telltale V-shaped wake which immediately appeared upon the surface. The wake was not produced by the ordinary slow swimming in which the porpoise indulged when not responding to acoustic stimulation. It was caused only when the speed of swimming was increased by the typical avoidance or startle response, which now became observable in this indirect manner.

The use of this cue to the change in swimming speed permitted the corroboration of the previous findings at Marineland and Bimini, although to slightly different limits. The Daytona Beach porpoise reacted without fail to all frequencies up to 50,000 cycles per second, and 75 per cent of the time to frequencies of 60,000 cycles per second; but the results were doubtful or negative at 70 kilocycles and above. Two possibilities suggest themselves as to why reactions were not obtained at higher levels, even though they occurred regularly at Bimini to stimuli of 70 and 80 kilocycles. (1) The soft character of the bottom at Daytona undoubtedly affected sound transmission by absorbing a greater portion of the sound energy than at Bimini. (2) The sensitivity of the porpoises, at these threshold levels, may also have been different.

TABLE 3

RANK OR ORDER OF CERTAIN ORGANISMS ACCORDING TO
UPPER FREQUENCY THRESHOLD

Rank	Organism	Upper Threshold	Investigator
1–3	Frog	10,000	Yerkes (1905)
1–3	Canary	10,000	Brand and P. P. Kellogg (1939)
1–3	Pigeon	10,000	Wever and Bray (1937)
4	Human (adult)	20,000	Woodworth and Schlossberg (1954)
5	Human (child)	23,000	Elder (1935)
6	Chimpanzee	26,000	Elder (1935)
7	Dog	35,000	Dworkin (1934)
8–9	White rat	40,000	Gould and Morgan (1941)
8–9	Moth	40,000	Frings and Frings (1957)
11	Katydid	45,000	Wever and Bray (1933)
12	Cat	50,000	Dworkin (1934)
13	Porpoise	80,000	W. N. Kellogg and Kohler (1953)
14	Mouse	95,000	Dice and Bartow (1952)
15	Bat	98,000	Galambos (1941)

cycles per sec.

RELATIONSHIP TO OTHER ANIMALS

The order or position in which these findings place the bottlenose dolphin with regard to acoustic sensitivity, in comparison with other organisms, can be seen from Table 3. The first column in the table gives the ranking or order of the organism listed in terms of the number of vibrations per second (as shown in the third column) to which it has been observed to respond. The names of the investigators reporting these results are shown in the fourth column. It will be noted that if the maximum finding of 80,000 cycles per second is taken, the porpoise is exceeded by only two other species in its responsiveness to high-frequency tones.

Chapter 7

Perception of Submerged Targets

One may think of the brain as an enormously complex electronic computer. Flowing into it is a continuous stream of neural impulses initiated in the receptors and transmitted via the sensory nerves. These impulses are decoded and sorted in the higher nerve centers. The process of classifying them and associating them with previously stored impulses is what is called perception.

An ordinary man is unable to perceive very much about his surroundings merely by listening to trains of echoes reflected from objects nearby. But the structure of the porpoise brain, the adaptation of the acoustic receptor, and the responsiveness to ultrasonic frequencies all point to a remarkable capacity in this direction. There can be no doubt that the bottlenose dolphin possesses a receiving mechanism which is quite sufficient to take care of its own echo-ranging signals. The next question is how to demonstrate its extraordinary perceptual ability of reacting to water-borne echoes.

A DOLPHIN LABORATORY

To investigate the question, we found it necessary to get porpoises under closer observation than had previously been possible. The way to discover more about their sonar, we argued, was not to study wild porpoises at sea. Nor was it to make sporadic observations of animals in public aquariums. We had to have some specimens of our own that we could study under controlled conditions. It would be difficult, if not impossible, to transport such large water-dwelling organisms into a standard acoustics laboratory. But we could build a special "porpoise laboratory," together with the proper equipment for working with them in their natural environment. It would be one of the few times (if not the first time) that a university had gone so far as to construct on its own property a special facility for the specific purpose of maintaining small whales (W. Kellogg, 1958*b*).

Many months of entreating, cajoling, and begging were required to raise the necessary funds and to obtain permission from the proper authorities to begin such a project. After that, over a year was taken up in its construction. Although the finished product cost more to build than a good-sized house, the result was well worth the effort. It consisted of a large outdoor pool or enclosure at the Marine Laboratories of Florida State University, 43 miles south of Tallahassee at Alligator Harbor on the Gulf Coast. The black mud or marl from which the pool was excavated gave soft, sound-absorbent sides and bottom. These were ideal for studies of echo-ranging, since they reflected few, if any, echoes themselves. They resembled what are known as anechoic surfaces.

The over-all dimensions of the enclosure were 70 by 55 feet, with a depth at low tide of 5.5 feet and a depth at high tide of about 7 feet. At the south end were two individual cells or

93

cages 15 by 25 feet, which could be closed by doors projecting above and below the water line (Fig. 8). Salt water was supplied through a sea wall, which protected the excavation from wave damage. A board walk was built around the edge of the pool at the water line, and a small dock protruded from the south bank.

To move apparatus or other accessories from one place to an-

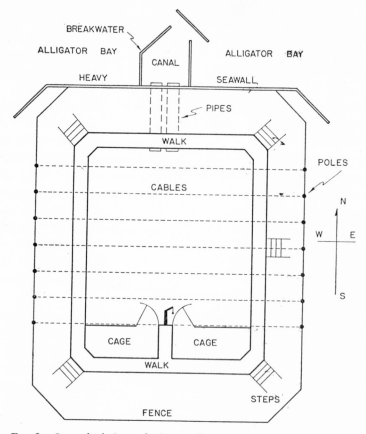

Fɪɢ. 8.—General design of the outdoor "porpoise laboratory." The dimensions of the pool were 55 by 70 feet. Overhanging cables between rows of telephone poles to the east and west were used for supporting underwater apparatus or partitions. A small crane or hoist to the south permitted lowering of heavy acoustical equipment.

other, either above or beneath the water, skiffs were available, and a small raft was built. Another device for handling apparatus was a crane or hoist which was mounted at the end of a short pier projecting into the pool from the south bank. Still a third method, which offered greater mobility, was a horizontal network of cables and wires.

Along each of the longer sides of the pool were rows of small telephone poles. The cables were stretched horizontally between these poles 10 to 15 feet above the water. From the cables we could lower plastic partitions, wire fencing, or underwater acoustical apparatus at any place in the pool. We could also haul observers out over the water in bosun's chairs.

Into these surroundings were placed two fine animals donated by the Marine Laboratories of Marineland, Florida. They were transported 260 miles by truck. With such facilities, we went to work in earnest. Assistants helped in building apparatus and accessories. Teams of graduate students donated their time to conduct special experiments. Professors in other disciplines generously contributed their knowledge. The purpose of all this was to get at the efficiency of the echo-ranging process.

ACOUSTICAL TECHNIQUES

First to be investigated were the reactions which the porpoises made to submerged targets of different size and shape. To this end, we set up acoustical equipment and kept a hydrophone almost constantly in the pool. Some of the hydrophones which were used in this work (a Navy type 3A and three type AX-58's) were loaned on contracts with the Office of Naval Research. Additional sound apparatus consisted of a Navy type 1K transducer or underwater speaker, tape recorders of different sorts, including an Ampex 307, Dumont oscilloscopes (Nos. 247 and 304H), a Grass oscilloscope camera, high-pass and adjustable band-pass filters, together with appropriate amplifiers, pre-amplifiers, power supplies, air speakers, and other electronic accessories. This equipment (exclusive of hydrophones) was

95

housed in an apparatus room in a laboratory building adjacent to the pool.

The acoustical apparatus was employed in the following ways:

1. It was set up for listening to the underwater noises made by the animals as reflecting targets were submerged. The sounds were picked up by a hydrophone and were sent through an air speaker so that human observers could hear them.

2. The sounds were recorded on the Ampex, or on other tape recorders, for subsequent analysis in the laboratory. (The Ampex 307 will record frequencies to 100 kc. $\pm$ 5 decibels.)

3. Porpoise sounds were also transmitted to a cathode-ray oscilloscope and were photographed directly by the Grass camera, or they were photographed from the tape play-back of the recorder. In some instances, listening, recording, and photographing were undertaken simultaneously.

In addition to the study of the sonar clicking responses, the ability of the animals to locate, approach, or avoid submerged targets was tested. The targets varied in size, shape, and solidity. The nature and description of the separate objects which were employed will be given later when the results for each target are discussed.

CONTROL OF VISUAL CUES

The possibility that vision was used by the animals in any of the tests was eliminated by the turbidity or opacity of the water within the porpoise enclosure. Shoal water in Alligator Harbor is cloudy and brownish from about April through November (depending on water temperature), although it clears somewhat during the winter months. This natural turbidity was augmented in the pool by the mud stirred up by porpoise swimming.

Measurements of turbidity were taken regularly with a 20-centimeter Secchi disc. The Secchi disc is a circular white reflecting surface which is submerged in a vertical direction until it becomes invisible. The point at which it disappears from view is measured in inches from the surface of the water. Since there is no turbidity in the air, a Secchi reading, in effect, gives the absolute visual threshold in inches from the eye of the observer. For the purposes of this investigation, divers also made Secchi measurements in a horizontal direction within the pool about one foot below the surface of the water. The horizontal thresholds obtained in this way were found to be about equal to the vertical readings. The transmission of light was further checked by transparency measurements of water samples with a photoelectric colorimeter. The results confirmed the Secchi readings.

During the months when the present observations were being made, the Secchi thresholds averaged 24.1 inches, with a standard deviation of 10.1 inches. Since the Secchi disc is a brilliant white, this means that black or neutral stimuli—like many of those used in these studies—would disappear from view at shorter distances. In this connection it should also be pointed out that a real question exists whether the eye of the porpoise is as good as that of man. Auditory reception is certainly far superior, but the visual mechanism may be less well developed (see chap. 6). Nevertheless, to insure a more than adequate margin of safety, test objects were immersed in the present instance from 8 to 50 feet from the position of the nearest porpoise. These targets were put in only when the animals were at rest—that is, in one position in the pool. As a final control on the remote possibility that vision played any part whatever in the reactions of the animals to submerged objects, some of the tests were conducted during the dark phase of the moon in almost complete darkness at night.

CHANGES IN THE SIGNAL

The sonar clicking sound was the basic auditory response which was made by the porpoises to the objects we immersed. Separate trains or bursts of these sound signals occurring in the pool would generally last from 1 to 5 seconds, although successive series might follow one another rapidly. The spacing or rate-per-second at which the individual pings took place within any given train or series varied considerably. This variation extended from a few to several hundred pulses per second.

The animals appeared to alter the spacing or timing of the pulses in accordance with what they were pinging or beaming on. Our observations suggest that the pulses occurred closer together if a porpoise swam toward a target after its immersion. In some cases, an animal would change the rate-per-second of the pulses within the limits of a single burst. If, for example, the clicks started slowly but accelerated in rate-per-second, they would be individually audible to human ears at first, but would lose their identity as the whole series took on a tonal quality of its own.

The subjects were also observed to control or modulate the intensity of the pulses in different testing situations. There was some evidence that they changed the intensity within a single burst or series of sound signals lasting but a few seconds. Hence, a given sequence might start loud and end weak, or vice versa. This was, of course, not always true; and, since acoustical determinations of this nature are necessarily a function of the recording system, the change in intensity may in some cases have been an artifact produced by the varying distance of the animal from the hydrophone. Yet, such changes also occurred when alterations in distance were not involved.

In general, our observations showed that the sonar sounds of the porpoise differed from man-made sonar in (*a*) the rate-per-second of the separate pings, (*b*) intensity modulation, and (*c*) frequency composition.

REACTIONS TO REFLECTING TARGETS

Perhaps the simplest method of eliciting the underwater sound clicks was to throw a pebble into the water. The noise of its splashing was followed immediately by one or more trains of pulses. Stronger splashes, such as those caused by a rock or a handful of pebbles, elicited louder and longer reactions.

Observations like these led to a systematic attempt to examine the effects on both the auditory response and the general behavior of the animals which might be produced by different sorts of sound-reflecting targets. Streamlined or tear-drop objects were therefore made which could be lowered slowly into the water at the end of a line without causing the slightest noise on immersion. Other targets were prepared which were intended to produce water noise or surface splashing. Whether or not any sound occurred on contact with the water was continuously monitored by underwater listening.

The shape and over-all dimensions of eight of these devices are diagramed in Figure 9. Items 1 and 6 in this figure were

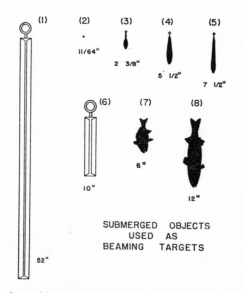

FIG. 9.—Various objects used as targets for testing the echo-ranging of porpoises. Items (*1*) and (*6*) are polelike sheet-metal devices, triangular in cross section; (*2*) represents a BB shot; and (*3*), (*4*), and (*5*) are streamlined shapes which could be silently lowered into the water without a splash. Other targets were fishes, notably the spot, *Leiostomus xanthurus* (*7*), and the mullet, *Mugel cephalus* (*8*).

made of 28-gauge sheet metal and were triangular in cross-section, 2 inches to the side. Item 2 represents a BB shot; 3, 4, and 5 are black streamlined shapes; and 7 and 8 represent food-fish chosen approximately in the lengths indicated.

TABLE 4

PORPOISE REACTIONS TO REFLECTING TARGETS

Nature of Target			Method of Immersion	Behavior of Animals	
Description	Color	Item No.		Sound Signals Emitted	Swimming Response
52-in. sheet-metal pole	Galvanized	1	Audible	Signals on immersion	None or avoidance
BB shot ...	Black	2	Audible	Signals follow splash	None
Wooden streamlined shapes ...	Black	3, 4, 5	Silent	Signals after immersion	None
10-in. sheet-metal shape	Galvanized	6	Silent and audible	Signals on immersion	None
Clear plastic sheet, 3 x 4½ ft. ..	Invisible	...	Left in for long periods	Signals increase near target	Avoidance
Food-fish ..	Brown and silver	7, 8	Silent and audible	Repeated signals	Approach
Human swimmer	Skin	...	Audible	More frequent with swimmer in pool	Avoidance

These eight targets together with additional stimuli not pictured in Figure 9 are listed in Table 4. The table also gives the responses which the various stimuli produced. The column headed "Item No." in the table refers to the numbered targets shown in Figure 9, while "Method of Immersion" indicates whether an object was submerged silently, i.e., without water noise, or audibly, i.e., with splashing or water noise. The last two targets in Table 4 may be considered "soft" targets in the sense that they absorb auditory vibrations better than the others. No change was noted in the character of the sonar response in such cases, although it may be assumed that the echoes returned would be different in frequency composition from those sent back by harder or more rigid reflecting surfaces. In some instances, targets were placed in the water from behind a plywood screen extending 22 inches above and 2 inches below the surface. This effectively concealed the movements of the experimenters from the porpoises.

SURFACE SPLASHES WITHOUT TARGETS

In order to discover the effect of splashing alone on the beaming or sonar responses of the animals, isolated splashing sounds were produced without the subsequent insertion of a target. The best method of accomplishing this was to drop measured quantities of water from known heights above the surface. The water was dropped by an assistant suspended over the center of the pool in a bosun's chair. Such tests were made in calm weather when there was no wind or water disturbance.

TABLE 5

REACTIONS TO SOUNDS OF SPLASHING WATER

Nature of Stimulus	Behavior of Animals	
	Sound Signals Emitted	Swimming Response
1 drop, from 5-ft. height ...	None	None
Half-spoonful or more	Single train of signals	None
Stream from ½-in. hose	Continuous signals—"alarm" whistling	Fear reaction—frantic swimming
Sudden rainstorm	Continuous signals—"alarm" whistling	Fear reaction—frantic swimming

The principal results are summarized in Table 5. It will be seen from this table that the noise made by a single drop of water from a height of approximately 5 feet was a below-threshold stimulus for porpoise sound pings. But a half-teaspoonful of water, and larger amounts, would invariably elicit the sonar response. A stream of water from the nozzle of a half-inch garden hose—played even momentarily upon the surface—produced great disturbance, loud sound signals, undulating porpoise "alarm" whistles, and "flight" swimming reactions.

On several occasions, a sudden shower came up while experimenters were working at the pool. The behavioral and acoustic responses were the same as with a hose—presumably because the relatively shallow depth of the pool allowed no escape from the din to deeper and quieter water.

It became clear from these observations that clicking noises could be triggered by splashes of almost any kind. But such responses were not sustained unless reflecting targets—from which echoes would return—were actually present after the splash. The "plunk" made by a single BB shot, for example, was sufficient to intitiate a train of signals. However, since the shot sank rapidly to the bottom, the sounds were soon discontinued.

SIGNIFICANT SONAR RESPONSES

Some special results which came to light during these tests were as follows:

1. Even though they remained in the same location within the pool, the animals emitted periodic trains of sound pulses every 15 or 20 seconds. These appeared to be exploratory pings equivalent to "glancing" or "peering" in the field of vision.

2. A food-fish silently immersed from behind a screen elicited no reaction until a train of exploratory beaming signals indicated its presence. Thereupon, the trains of echo-ranging noises became almost continuous as the porpoise approached and took the bait. Since an animal usually lay at or near the top of the water during feeding, it could clearly be seen to lurch or jerk forward by giving a powerful movement of its horizontal tail flukes the moment echoes were received. It obviously "knew" that a food-fish had been inserted, even though visual perception was impossible because of the turbidity of the water.

3. In swimming toward a small target, such as food-fish held beneath the water, a porpoise could often be seen to move its

head and trunk alternately to the right and left. Movements of this nature have been reported in a single captive specimen by Schevill and Lawrence (1956) and were described in two additional animals by W. Kellogg (1958*a*, 1960).

Oscillating head movements occurred only (*a*) while the animal was emitting trains of sound pulses and (*b*) when the target toward which it was swimming could not be visually identified because of the turbidity of the water. Observations of this phenomenon indicate that a complete cycle takes place in from 2 to 3 seconds. The oscillating activity was noted at distances up to 10 feet from the target, and it continued until the dolphin got close enough to seize or take the food.

Moving the target slowly in a direction perpendicular to the porpoise's line of approach caused the animal to turn continuously so as to keep the target in the median plane. There was no interruption in the angular oscillations under such conditions. If the target was moved rapidly, there was an appreciable and clearly observable latency in the orienting behavior which resulted. The aim of the porpoise lagged behind the actual position of the target at any instant. If the direction of movement of the target was abruptly reversed, the animal would overshoot the turning point (W. Kellogg, 1960).

The speed of forward motion in such cases was calculated for one animal and was found to be quite slow. In 172 measurements made over a period of four weeks, it averaged 0.34 feet per second. (The average of 0.34 feet per second is roughly equivalent to 0.2 miles per hour.) The magnitude of the oscillation of the head and body was estimated at about 10 degrees, or 5 degrees on either side of the median plane. What takes place in such instances is diagramed schematically in Figure 10.

THE MEANING OF THE OSCILLATIONS

The only adequate interpretation of this activity appears to be that it is a means of orientation to the echoes of the sound signals which are reflected back from the target. The original sound

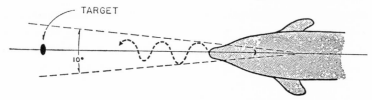

Fɪɢ. 10.—Auditory scanning in the bottlenose dolphin. When echolocating a small target such as fish, the porpoise approaches by oscillating its head to the right and left through an arc of about 10 degrees. This behavior undoubtedly includes binaural localization as well as echolocation.

pulses broadcast by the dolphin do not appear to be highly directional—probably no more so than the human voice. But the echoes returning from an object at a fixed point in space would vary continuously as the locus of the animal's ears changed with reference to the source of the echoes.

The oscillation of the head is exactly what one would expect in the pinpointing of an object by means of reflected sound. It is the same sort of activity in which a human being would engage if he were using binaural localization. The head move-

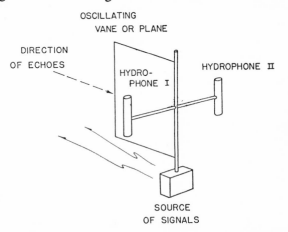

Fɪɢ. 11.—In order to duplicate mechanically the auditory scanning of the porpoise, it would be necessary to have parts somewhat like these diagramed above. Left out of account in such a scheme is the electronic computer necessary to decode and analyze the echoes.

ments of the animal would constantly modulate the phase and intensity differences of the echoing sound waves reaching each of the ears. They would also alter the time interval between the emission of a pulse signal and the return of its echo to each ear. The continuation of the process as the porpoise swam forward would enable it to determine with great precision the direction from which the echoes came.

AUDITORY SCANNING

Since the noises which make up the echoes are emitted by the animal itself, the activity as a whole amounts to a kind of scanning by sound. We suggest, therefore, the term "auditory scanning" as a good name for both the acoustic and the general behavior comprising this elaborate pattern of activity. The analogy with optics is enhanced if auditory scanning is compared to visual scanning conducted at night with the aid of a light.

Auditory scanning may be thought of as more complex than visual scanning, for it represents a combination of two already complex processes. Auditory scanning consists of (*a*) the emission of a continuous series of sound signals for the purpose of echolocation and (*b*) binaural localization. It might be characterized as "binaural-echo-localization."

Above and beyond this activity is the perceptual process itself. The stream of information produced by auditory scanning must be instantly analyzed by the amazing brain of the animal. The mechanical counterpart of such a receptor system would be a sonar apparatus with one transmitter and two independent receivers, plus an electronic computer capable of decoding and processing the data—all within a single compact unit. Some of these devices are schematically represented in Figure 11.

Chapter 8

Distinguishing between Objects

We have agreed on three basic steps, it will be recalled, as necessary to establish the existence of porpoise sonar beyond any reasonable doubt. The first of these was to analyze the signal in order to see whether it met the requirements for echo-ranging in water; this is essentially the problem of transmission. The second was to study the acoustic sense in order to find out whether its design seemed adequate for the decoding and analysis of the reflected echoes; this is the problem of reception. Each of these problems has been dealt with in an earlier chapter. Having determined that the mechanisms of transmission and reception are not only adequate but in fact astonishingly complex, we are now safe in concluding that the porpoise possesses an excellent sonar system.

But such a conclusion does not solve the issue. Instead, it leads to the most difficult problem of all. For, even though the dolphin has a fine sonar system, it still remains to be demonstrated that the system is actually used for orientation and navigation. Do porpoises employ it in a positive way to seek and find food-objects like fish? Do they employ it in a negative way to avoid obstacles or obstructions while swimming?

In chapter 7, a beginning was made with regard to this last problem by finding out how dolphins react to reflecting targets which are placed in the water near them. From the patterns of sound signals and the general behavior which resulted, we decided that these animals "see with their ears" in a way comparable to the perceptual process of seeing with the eye. Schevill and Lawrence (1956) have also contributed to the solution of this problem by observing how a porpoise acts when it is fed. But the results of these studies do not tell us nearly enough. We must consequently go deeper into the question and try to discover more specifically (*a*) just what it is that porpoises "see" and (*b*) just how well they "see" it. The remainder of the book will be devoted principally to the answers to these questions. In the present chapter, we shall take up the problem of size discrimination, namely, the ability to distinguish between targets of different areas (W. Kellogg, 1959*b*).

RACING FOR A FISH

At the laboratory in Alligator Bay each porpoise was fed daily from 15 to 18 pounds of fresh (frozen, but defrosted) fish. The fish were either thrown into the pool one at a time or fed to the animals directly from the hand. Suppose that a food-fish is thrown into the turbid water of the porpoise enclosure in such a way as to strike the water 30 feet or so from the two experimental animals. If the test is to be critical, the animals should neither be able to see the fish in the air nor should they be able to see the motions of the thrower. The instant the bait strikes the water, both porpoises immediately turn and race toward it at a maximum speed, although, before they can arrive at the spot, the fish, if fresh, will have sunk beneath the surface.

The bait is by then not visible to human observers on the bank, nor to the animals. Yet one or the other of them never fails to retrieve it and usually surfaces almost immediately with the fish in its mouth. The whole procedure takes but a few seconds. There is no exploratory or searching behavior whatever. It is clear, of course, that the sound of the splash gives the direction for swimming. But the sonar process is undoubtedly used in finding the fish after it sinks.

Can senses other than audition be used for locating such a submerged target? Obviously, the method of discovery cannot be a visual one in extremely turbid water. It cannot be olfactory, for we know that the sense of smell is missing in these animals (Haan, 1957, p. 20). Gustatory reception seems highly improbable in such a situation, for the chase and seizure of the sinking fish are much too fast for any tasting to take place. The response is like that of a dog picking up a stick on the run. There remain the tactual and temperature senses, and audition. We are forced by the process of elimination to infer again that the acoustic receptor must be the sensory channel which is employed.

PREFERENCES IN DIET

At first, our two subjects were fed on mullet, *Mugil cephalus* (Linnaeus), but they soon began to refuse this fish. It therefore became necessary to supply them with a fish called spot, *Leiostomus xanthurus* (Lacépède), which they ate readily. Either of these food-fishes held by the tail beneath the surface of the water would be approached from distances well beyond the range of visibility. Upon contact with a mullet, however, a porpoise would reject it; but the spot would be seized and eaten. A similar distinction existed when the fishes were thrown into the water at a point distant from an animal's position. Both spot and mullet would be actively chased, but the mullet was almost never taken.

As a consequence of this behavior, the question arose whether the animals could discriminate between a preferred fish (the spot) and a non-preferred fish (the mullet) without seeing either fish. The sonar process would then have to be used as the method of selection. With the use of this natural preference as a basis for approaching and avoiding behavior, a choice or discrimination experiment was consequently arranged to which proper experimental controls could be applied. The discriminating cues were differences in the sizes of the preferred and non-preferred stimuli. To this end, mullet which were about twice as large in over-all length as the spot were selected for the experiment. The subject of the experiment was Albert, a young and vigorous adolescent. Albert was over 7 feet long and weighed in the neighborhood of 300 pounds.

THE METHOD OF TESTING

Twenty-four inches from the end of a 30-inch-wide dock or pier which protruded 15 feet into the water at one end of the pool, was placed a rectangular sheet of $\frac{5}{16}$-inch marine plywood, 24 by 48 inches. The plywood was mounted perpendicular to the end of the dock, in a vertical plane and with its longer axis horizontal. It was fastened on brackets, so that it could be raised or lowered with changes in the tidal level. The height of the plywood was adjusted during an experimental session to bring its lower edge 1 to 2 inches beneath the surface. This left a vertical screen, 48 by 22–23 inches, in the air above the water. From behind the screen, target-fishes could be submerged without giving any visual cues to the subject.

A team of two experimenters was required for the daytime sessions and three for the night sessions. In presenting the fishes to the subject, it was necessary for Experimenter 1 (E1) to lie prone upon the dock with arms and shoulders protruding over its end, although still behind the screen. Experimenter 2 (E2) was stationed behind E1 with a stopwatch and recording material. A sound-powered telephone system used at night connected E2 to an adjacent building where E3, working under a dim screened light, recorded data which were relayed from the pool.

Underwater acoustical and electronic equipment like that described earlier (W. Kellogg, 1959*a*; Kellogg *et al.,* 1953) was also employed during many of the sessions. This was used to listen to the porpoise's sound signals as it approached the stimuli.

At the beginning of a trial, E1 simultaneously lowered a positive and a negative stimulus (a spot and a mullet) into the water. A fish was held by the tail in each hand, so that both the tail and the hand were concealed behind the lower edge of the plywood screen. The points of insertion were 24 inches apart and were fixed with reference to the vertical edges of the screen. The distance of immersion was about 6 inches for the spot and about 12 inches for the mullet, measured from the bottom or submerged edge of the plywood. The positions of the positive and negative stimuli were randomly rotated from trial to trial.

The general arrangement of the screen and target fishes is diagramed in Figure 12. This plan, it will be seen, presented the porpoise with a size-discrimination problem. The positive

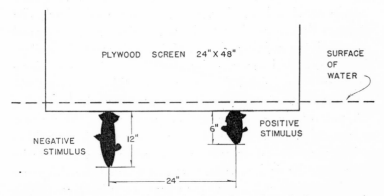

Fig. 12.—Arrangement of the stimuli to determine whether a porpoise can discriminate between underwater targets of different sizes by echo-ranging. Neither stimulus is visible to the subject because of the turbidity or opacity of the water.

stimulus (the spot) offered a smaller reflecting surface to the animal than the negative stimulus (the mullet). It was the subject's task to approach and take the spot and at the same time to avoid the mullet—without employing vision in the selective process. Albert was about 23 hours hungry at the start of any experimental session.

TIMING AND DURATION OF TRIALS

A trial began when the subject was completely "ready." Being "ready" consisted of the animal's coming to the top of the water and maintaining a fixed position several feet in front of the plywood screen. In such cases, the porpoise stopped swimming and lay upon the surface, waiting or "treading water." Its dorsal fin remained above the water, and the top of its head would alternately rise and fall a few inches every 5 or 10 seconds as it came up to breathe or blow. E1 immersed the two fishes at the instant the porpoise was in the process of blowing or exhaling. The fish were inserted head downward and with complete silence. Any uncontrolled water noise which occurred inadvertently on immersion, was adequately masked by the "whoosh" of the animal's blowing.

At the moment of immersion, E1 quietly said, "In." Upon this signal E2 began to time the trial. Two independent time measurements were recorded, each of which began at the start of the trial. When the subject touched a fish with its nose or mouth, E1 said, "Contact." When Albert took the bait from E1's hand, E1 said, "Take." E1 could tell by touch—both in daytime and in the night sessions—the instant Albert contacted or took either fish.

The minimum interval between trials was approximately 1 minute, although the intertrial interval was occasionally lengthened by Albert to as long as 15 minutes. Frequently the porpoise swam about the pool, sometimes with the fish in its mouth, during the first part of the intertrial interval. Obviously, the next trial could not begin until Albert was "ready."

STARTING POSITION

Because the porpoise did most of its approaching at or very near the surface, it was not difficult for observers on the dock above to tell its position with reference to the target fishes, despite the turbidity of the water. At the same time, the animal could not detect the stimuli by visual means because of this turbidity. The situation, in fact, possessed some of the characteristics of a one-way-vision screen, the advantage being all in favor of the experimenters. The diagram in Figure 13 should make this clear.

Since the starting point with reference to the screen on any given trial was actually determined by the porpoise, it was, of course, somewhat variable. Consequently, estimates of the starting distance and of the angle of approach were recorded by E2 during all but the first two daytime sessions. These permitted calculations of the speed or rate of approach in estimated feet-per-second for each trial.

TRIALS PER SESSION

Fourteen experimental sessions of this sort were conducted. These sessions were distributed irregularly—because of weather and other conditions—over a period of about six weeks. Between sessions, Albert was fed by hand, but without the necessity of discriminating between preferred and non-preferred fishes. From fourteen to twenty-seven discrimination trials were given at a session, the exact number depending on the strength of the subject's hunger drive. When Albert stopped getting ready or refused to approach the feeding station, a session was necessarily terminated. The experiment was not begun until after the porpoise had become thoroughly habituated to the situation and had had more than four months' experience taking food-fish from human attendants.

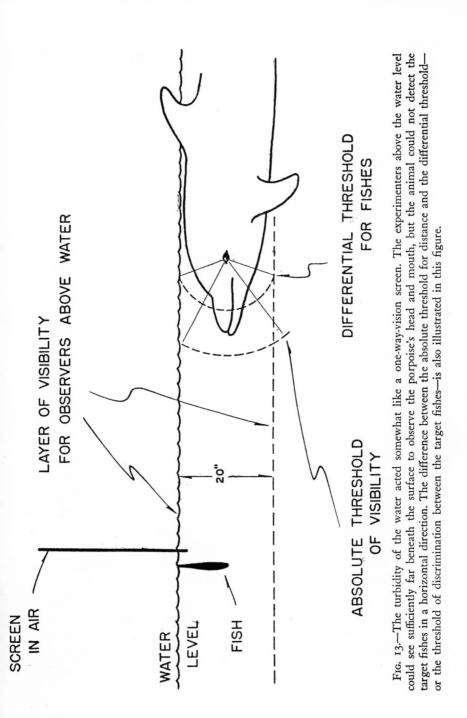

SCREEN
IN AIR

LAYER OF VISIBILITY
FOR OBSERVERS ABOVE WATER

WATER
LEVEL

FISH

20"

ABSOLUTE THRESHOLD
OF VISIBILITY

DIFFERENTIAL THRESHOLD
FOR FISHES

FIG. 13.—The turbidity of the water acted somewhat like a one-way-vision screen. The experimenters above the water level could see sufficiently far beneath the surface to observe the porpoise's head and mouth, but the animal could not detect the target fishes in a horizontal direction. The difference between the absolute threshold for distance and the differential threshold—or the threshold of discrimination between the target fishes—is also illustrated in this figure.

THE ELIMINATION OF VISION

In any study of echo-ranging or echolocation, it is absolutely essential that uncontrolled visual cues be permanently and completely eliminated. This was brought about in the present instance by the turbidity or opacity of the water in the porpoise pool and the consequent low degree of light penetration. As in the case of the observations discussed in chapter 7, both vertical and horizontal measurements of the turbidity of the water were also taken throughout the present experiment. The horizontal readings were made by skin divers. A Secchi disc, employed in these measurements, gave absolute thresholds of visibility in terms of inches of distance from the eye of the observer.

Similar determinations were made of the maximum horizontal distance, under the water, from which it was possible for a skin diver to distinguish between a 12-inch mullet and a 6-inch spot. Such measurements were, in effect, differential or discrimination thresholds in terms of inches. The discrimination thresholds were found to be 40 to 50 per cent of the absolute Secchi readings. This meant that a Secchi measurement of 20 inches read from the surface downward could be translated into a skin diver's differential threshold between the two fishes of 8 or 10 inches. The manner in which this turbidity affected the visual capacity of the porpoise is shown schematically in Figure 13.

The results of many of these measurements of visibility are given in Table 6, together with relevant data on the estimated starting position from which the porpoise began its approach to the stimuli. To simplify comparisons, all linear data are given in feet or fractions thereof. It will be noted from Table 6 that the average Secchi threshold (col. 1) was 1.57 feet or about 19 inches. But the discrimination threshold for spot and mullet of different sizes in every case was less than one-half (about 40 per cent) of the absolute thresholds. This means that, if a human observer could detect anything (for example, the Secchi disc) from a distance of 19 inches, he could not see well enough in

TABLE 6

VISIBILITY (TURBIDITY) MEASUREMENTS OF WATER IN FEET

Session No.	Absolute Visibility Threshold (1)	Approximate Discrimination Threshold (2)	Average Distance between Start and Goal (3)	Minimum Distance on Any Trial (3)	Visual Margin of Safety (4/2)
1	1.42	0.7	N.R.	N.R.	...
2	1.42	0.7	N.R.	N.R.	...
3	1.67	0.8	4.7	4	5.0
4	1.67	0.8	5.6	3	3.8
5	1.42	0.7	5.4	4	5.7
6	1.42	0.7	6.3	5	7.1
7	1.71	0.9	5.1	4	4.4
8	1.58	0.8	5.5	3	3.8
9	1.58	0.8	5.3	3	3.8
10 * ..	...	...	...	...	...
11 ...	1.67	0.8	3.4	3	3.8
12 * ..	...	...	...	...	...
13 ...	1.67	0.8	4.2	4	5.0
14 ...	N.R.	N.R.	4.8	2	...
Average	1.57	0.8	5.0	3.5	4.7

N.R. = not recorded.
* Night sessions.

this degree of turbidity to tell which of the two fishes was larger than the other until he had approached to within 7 or 8 inches of the stimuli to be discriminated. Differential limens were not measured at every session, although enough were obtained to establish the approximate 40 per cent relationship between the differential and the lower or absolute limen. In order to "err in the right direction," however, DL's computed on the basis of a full 50 per cent of the corresponding Secchi readings are presented in Table 6 (col. 2) for comparative purposes.

Columns 3 and 4 show the average and the minimum estimated starting distances of the animal for all trials of the sessions indicated. If we take the minimum (not the average) and compare it to the discrimination thresholds in column 2, the margins of safety obtained in the last column of the table are obtained. The smallest of these, it appears, is 3.8 times larger than necessary, and the largest is more than 7 times as big as it needs to be.

THE EYE-NOSE DISTANCE

Another and equally convincing approach to this question can be made through the medium of porpoise anatomy. The distance from the end of a porpoise's beak (or mouth) to the eye is ⅙ to ⅐ of the total body length. In porpoises of Albert's dimensions, the distance from the anterior protrusion of the lower jaw to the retina would consequently be 12 to 14 inches (1.00 to 1.17 feet). It should be noted, however, that the subject took fish from the hand of the person doing the feeding very gently and with its front teeth. The distance from its eyes to the bait at the moment of closing the jaws would therefore have been greater in every case than the estimated discrimination thresholds in Table 6. It seems reasonable to conclude that the animal could never have seen a fish well enough to identify

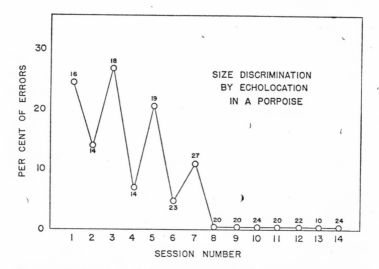

FIG. 14.—Performance of the porpoise in the size-discrimination situation diagramed in Figure 12. The numbers above each point indicate the number of discrimination trials determining that point.

it by vision—if indeed it could be seen at all—*even at the moment of seizure.* Nevertheless, identification of the correct fish most certainly occurred. And, in most instances, it appeared to have been made by the time the subject began moving forward from a starting position several feet away.

We should add, finally, that the sensitivity of the porpoise eye quite likely is no better than the sensitivity of the human eye and may, in fact, be inferior (Haan, 1957, p. 20; R. Kellogg, 1928). The human readings given in Table 6 are therefore quite safe as applied to porpoise vision. There would seem to be no possibility that the visual receptor could have played any part whatever in the ability of the animal to discriminate between the positive and negative stimuli.

DISCRIMINATION BY SOUND

The percentage of incorrect choices, or errors, made by the subject in the 271 trials of this experiment have been plotted for each session in Figure 14. Errors represent trials in which the negative fish (or mullet) was either touched or taken. It is apparent from the nature of this curve that some learning took place, although the largest percentage of errors in any one session was no more than 28. This relatively low error score indicates the degree of discrimination which was present from the very beginning—even in the artificial and unnatural situation of the experiment. In the last 7 sessions (8 through 14), totaling 140 trials, there occurred not a single incorrect choice.

Since porpoises are naturally timid in the presence of strange objects, the improvement in performance may be attributed in part to adaptation to the screen and to the experimental environment. However, it can also be explained as the building-up of an association or conditioned response. If one uses the conditioning paradigm, the unconditioned or reinforcing stimulus may be thought of as the taste or touch of the positive fish, and the conditioned stimulus as the pattern of echoes reflected by the positive fish.

TIME AND SPEED OF SWIMMING

Both "contact" and "take" times, it will be recalled, were tabulated for each trial. "Contact" time is the interval between the beginning of a trial and the porpoise's first physical contact with the bait. "Take" time is the interval between the start of a trial and the final removal of the fish from the hand of the experimenter. These times, as averaged for each session, are given in Table 7. The correlation coefficient (rho) between contact and take times per session was + 0.85. The average contact time per session for the experiment as a whole was 7.9 ± 1.8 second, and the average take time was 8.4 ± 1.6 second. The difference of 0.5 second between the averages was not statistically significant—a result to be expected under the present conditions.

TABLE 7

AVERAGE RESPONSE TIMES FOR CORRECT TRIALS IN SECONDS

Session No.	Average Contact Time	Average Take Time	Difference
1	7.17	8.00	0.83
2	6.92	9.17	2.25
3	5.25	6.42	1.17
4	6.29	7.71	1.42
5	6.36	6.64	0.28
6	8.52	8.76	0.24
7	8.45	8.50	0.05
8	7.47	8.16	0.69
9	6.65	6.80	0.15
10 *	7.04	7.50	0.46
11	11.25	11.40	0.15
12 *	8.41	8.50	0.09
13	12.20	12.20	0.00
14	8.29	8.29	0.00

* Night sessions.

Perhaps the most important of the time data were the differences between the contact and take times for the individual sessions. These differences have been charted in Figure 15. In the early trials, there was a considerable interval between the moment the animal touched the bait and the moment it was taken, while in the last two sessions, this time lag reduced to zero. The gradual decrease between the contact and take times, following the form of a typical learning curve, may again be described as a decrease in hesitancy or hesitation on the part of the porpoise. Or, it may be interpreted as evidence of the strengthening or improvement of the conditioned response. In the early trials, the reflected sound pattern from the spot (conditioned stimulus) had to be reinforced by contact or taste (unconditioned stimulus) before Albert would make the consummatory reaction of taking the spot. In the last two sessions, the sound pattern alone was sufficient to elicit the final response without intermediate gustatory reinforcement

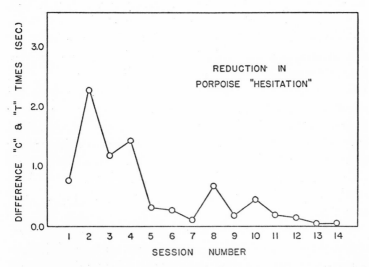

Fig. 15.—Average difference in seconds between "contact" and "take" times for correct discrimination trials.

By dividing the average distance of approach (col. 3, Table 6) by the average contact time for each session (Table 7), it is possible to compute the approximate speed of approach in feet-per-second. The rate of swimming toward the targets was found by this method to be surprisingly slow. It ranged from 0.9 feet per second to 0.3 feet per second—or approximately 0.6 to around 0.2 miles per hour—the speed *reducing* as the trials progressed.

EVIDENCE OF ECHOLOCATION

That the discrimination was actually accomplished by echo-ranging and not through some other sensory means was confirmed in three distinct ways.

1. The first of these was the altered pattern of sound pings which occurred after the immersion of the target fishes. Underwater acoustical gear permitted observers to listen to the audible component of the animal's noises as the sounds were being produced on any given trial. Typically, Albert sent out intermittent bursts or trains of sonar pulses (Kellogg *et al.*, 1953) while waiting at the "ready" or starting point. The first series of signals which occurred after the immersion of the stimuli—that is, the first series which would return echoes from the fishes—was accompanied by a forward lunge as the porpoise suddenly moved his powerful tail flukes. A start toward the goal was never made during a silent period between trains of signals. As the animal approached and took the bait, the pinging sound-trains became continuous, or nearly continuous. Moreover, the porpoise would sometimes oscillate its head to the right and left in approaching a fish, as porpoises are known to do in pinpointing a target (see chap. 7).

2. From Table 6, it will be seen that sessions 10 and 12 were conducted at night. The night sessions were scheduled when there was no moon. It was a fortunate coincidence that, on both occasions, the sky was heavily overcast so that starlight was also eliminated. The experimenters on the dock could tell when Albert was ready for a trial by the repeated breathing or blowing noises from a fixed position in front of the experimental screen. The data were communicated by telephone to a recorder or third experimenter located some distance away in a blacked-out building.

The discriminating ability of the animal under these night-time conditions was quite the same as in the daylight. The lack of illumination did not disturb the efficiency of performance (Fig. 14), nor did it alter the subject's behavior in any observable manner. The magnitude of the response times for sessions 10 and 12 was not noticeably affected, nor were the differences between the contact and the take times (Fig. 15). Visual perception in the turbid water of the pool would most certainly have been reduced—if not eliminated completely—in such darkness. Echolocation or auditory perception, on the other hand, would remain unchanged.

3. Two supplementary control sessions (not treated in the tables or the figures) were given in daylight at the end of the experiment. In these new trials, a 6-inch spot was paired with a mullet which was now held, like the spot, so as to protrude *only 6 inches below the plywood screen.* The two stimuli, in other words, were in this case of approximately the same size. In the first control session of 10 trials Albert made 2 errors. In the second session of 20 trials there were 10 errors. Combining the results of these two sessions gives a total of 40 per cent errors for the 30 control trials. Yet, in well over 100 previous trials when the positive and negative stimuli had differed in size, the subject had committed no errors at all (Fig. 14). Elimination of the size differential had obviously disrupted or destroyed the discrimination.

These facts would seem to demonstrate conclusively (*a*) that the discrimination was made on the basis of size and (*b*) that it was made by echo-ranging.

SUBMARINES AND WHALES

Can a dolphin distinguish between separate objects *of the same area* but of different material? Two species of fish of the same size may not be easy to discriminate. This we have seen from the tests just described. Let us suppose, however, that a porpoise were called upon to tell the difference between two targets exactly alike in size and shape but constructed of basically different substances. What would happen, for example, if it had to distinguish a circular target 6 inches in diameter made of wood from a circular target 6 inches in diameter made of metal?

This is exactly the problem that has confronted man-made sonar. Not only have sonar men confused steel ships with wooden ships, but whales have often been mistaken for submarines. Yet whale blubber is vastly different in its compressibility and absorption characteristics from the unyielding hull of a vessel. Even if a submarine were as small as a whale (which is unlikely), there are fundamental differences in the surfaces of the two. Why is it that the echoes reflected to the sonar operator give little indication of this difference?

The porpoise can easily perceive a distinction between objects of this sort. At the Pacific Oceanarium Dr. Kenneth Norris offered a bottlenose porpoise a plastic capsule filled with water and a piece of fish of about the same dimensions. The animal consistently ignored the capsule but took the fish. After our size-discrimination experiment with spot and mullet had been completed, several control tests were made with the flat surface of the human hand. A hand 6 or 7 inches long presents roughly the same area as a spot. The spot was lowered in one position behind the visual screen, and the hand was simultaneously lowered at the other. In no case was the hand ever approached.

QUALITATIVELY DIFFERENT ECHOES

The process by which such a distinction is accomplished can perhaps be understood by comparing it to vision or to optics. Daylight or white light contains all the wave lengths of the visible spectrum. Yet, when white light is used to illuminate a red surface, red light is all that is reflected back. The same white signal reflects only green from a green surface, blue from a blue surface, and so on. The remaining wave lengths from the original light source are absorbed by their respective targets. The "coefficients of reflection" of the various surfaces are not the same.

The acoustic process of the porpoise follows exactly the same principle. Its sonar signals, like white light, send a wide band of wave lengths to the target. A series of porpoise clicks, as noted in chapter 5, is similar to "white noise." Some of the original frequencies transmitted by the animal are absorbed and some are reflected. Exactly which ones make up the returning echoes in any given instance is determined by the absorption and reflecting characteristics of the target. The echoes from different materials would therefore differ in composition or in quality. They would vary in the pattern of frequencies which they contain.

It has been shown, for example, that living tissue will absorb sound vibrations in different degrees according to the sonic and ultrasonic frequencies of the signal (Von Gierke *et al.*, 1952). Different sorts or kinds of living tissue are also known to have distinctive absorption coefficients. They would consequently reflect sound waves in a different manner. In the same way, the frequency composition of the echoes from a wooden surface would vary from the frequency composition of the echoes from a metal surface. Wood, in other words, simply "sounds different" from metal to a porpoise, in the same way that it looks different to the human eye. It is the sound spectrum of the returning vibrations which gives the clue to the nature of the reflecting surface.

The receptor system of the porpoise must be capable of perceiving and immediately reacting to distinctive auditory patterns of this sort. In effect, its acoustic analyzer performs a kind of frequency analysis for every echo which is received.

Chapter 9

The Avoidance of Invisible Barriers

Investigations which attempt to show that an organism can locate objects in its environment by listening to the echoes reflected from those objects must be so designed that the experimental subject has no opportunity to make use of optical cues in finding the target-stimuli. With the bottlenose dolphin, the method most commonly employed has been to conduct the tests in turbid water of low visibility (W. Kellogg, 1959a, 1959b; Schevill and Lawrence, 1956; see also chap. 8). Such a procedure assumes that a reduction in the penetration of light beneath the surface of the water effectively prevents any visual perception. However, the possibility that this basic assumption may be incorrect is always present in such studies. Their results would be less open to question if they were corroborated by a different methodological technique.

One might ask why the optic nerves of a research porpoise could not be cut, or the eyes surgically removed—a method which is used with smaller and less expensive laboratory animals. In the case of the porpoise, however, there are two real difficulties in the way of such a drastic procedure: (1) The bottlenose dolphin cannot be readily anesthetized for surgery, at least by conventional methods (see chap. 6). (2) How well a surgically mutilated porpoise would co-operate in research studies is also open to question. With such sensitive and intelligent animals, there would be a risk of abnormal behavior, as in the case of Betty in the approach-avoidance situation (chap. 2). Dr. Kenneth Norris has succeeded in blindfolding a captive dolphin by placing plastic or rubber suction cups over each eye. The method appears to work well, although it demands preliminary training and a high degree of co-operation on the part of the animal. The fundamental objective of all these procedures is simply to prevent the use of the visual receptor.

THE PARADOXICAL METHOD

There exists, however, an entirely different approach to the problem—a way of *controlling* vision without *eliminating* it at all. Under this new procedure, the animal would be permitted, or even encouraged, to see. As specifically applied in our studies, the technique was designed to give results which were different if the porpoise used vision from those which occurred if echolocation was employed. There is no need with such a method to blindfold the animal or to enucleate the eyes; and the water can remain perfectly clear, if so desired.

This new method of controlling vision should perhaps be characterized as "the paradoxical method" or as "the false-cue method." In the present instance, it was planned so as to confound the visual modality by offering erroneous or incorrect visual stimuli. The arrangement was such that optical cues were pitted against auditory cues. The use of vision was specifically permitted, therefore, in order to assess its value in the test situation. Both visual stimuli and acoustic echoes were simultaneously present, but they gave conflicting or contradictory information. The porpoise could be fooled or tricked if it responded visually, but not if it responded to the echoes of its own sonar signals. Consequently, the extent to which (*a*) vision and (*b*) echo-ranging were employed could be determined from the nature of the responses which were made.

In this new study, it was Albert again who was the subject of the investigation.

ACCESSIBLE AND INACCESSIBLE FISH

The secret of the method as used in this experiment was to offer the porpoise two desirable or preferred food-fish, both of which were spot (*Leiostomus xanthurus*). Each fish was identical in visual appearance. One of the fish, however, was always offered behind a solid sheet of ¼-inch plate glass. It was consequently inaccessible or unavailable. The other was free to be taken by the porpoise. The experiment was, in fact, a new sort of discrimination experiment, but in this case there could be no possibility of the discriminating response occurring through vision. The presence or absence of the screening sheet of glass could be detected from a distance only by echo-ranging. The unavailable spot (behind glass) was the negative stimulus, and the available spot was the positive stimulus. The general arrangement for producing this result is diagramed in Figure 16. We shall name this experiment "the glass-barrier experiment."

A rectangular metal frame of ³⁄₁₆-by-1½-inch angle iron was hung by a cable from a crane at the end of the 15-foot dock projecting into the porpoise pool. The frame, 60 inches long and 30 inches high, was bisected vertically to form two openings or windows 30 inches square. In addition to support from above, the frame was clamped to wooden brackets on the dock which held it rigidly in one position. It was adjusted so that its lower portion (about 20 inches) was beneath the water and the remainder in the air. That part of the apparatus above the surface (and about 2 inches below) was concealed from the subject by a plywood screen.

A 30-inch-square sheet of ¼-inch plate glass was fitted into

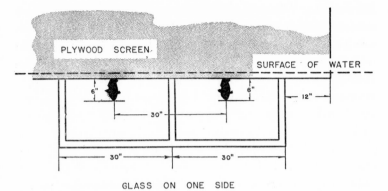

FIG. 16.—Apparatus used in the glass-barrier experiment. The porpoise was required to distinguish between two fish (spot) which were identical in visual appearance. The fish were presented simultaneously, but one was behind a sheet of plate glass. The glass was randomly shifted between the right and left windows.

this metal rectangle so as to slide to the right or left, thereby closing or blocking either half of the frame. The animal was thus faced with a discrimination apparatus consisting of two submerged apertures or windows, one of which was opened and the other closed. This arrangement permitted the simultaneous presentation of the two visually identical food-fish in the center of the two windows. The position of the glass was randomly changed from right to left upon successive trials.

As in previous experiments, underwater acoustical gear was continuously available for converting the water-borne noises of the animal into air signals which could be monitored by observers. By this means, any alterations in the sound pulses emitted by the porpoise as it performed in the experiment could be heard and also recorded on magnetic tape for subsequent study.

PRESENTING THE STIMULI

Three experimenters were required for the daytime sessions and four for those conducted at night. Experimenter 1 (E1) was located about 6 feet from the end of the dock with stop watch and recording materials. Two other experimenters (E2 and E3) handled the fishes which were used as stimuli. They lay prone, side by side, upon the dock in front of E1. Their shoulders and arms protruded over the end of the dock, but were nevertheless concealed from the porpoise behind the plywood screen. From this position, each lowered one of the target fishes into the water. The fourth experimenter (E4) remained during the nighttime sessions in a blacked-out laboratory building adjacent to the pool. Here he recorded data which were quietly relayed by sound-powered telephone from E1.

The fishes used as stimuli were held by the tail so as to project approximately 6 inches beneath the bottom edge of the ply-wood. The tail of each fish and the hands of the experimenters were hidden from the subject because of the screen. Both fish were placed in the water the same distance behind the apparatus. The two stimuli, in other words, were kept in the same vertical plane, which was parallel to and equidistant from the metal framework.

A trial began when the animal's behavior indicated it was ready. The porpoise would stop swimming and remain in a fixed position a few feet in front of the apparatus, "treading water" at the surface. As the animal exposed its blowhole to breathe in this position, E1 signaled E2 and E3 to immerse the fish. The timing of a trial began at this point. A trial would end when the porpoise touched or took the positive stimulus or bumped the glass or approached very close to the negative stimulus. Care was taken to submerge the target fishes silently, i.e., without splashing or water noise. Any uncontrolled water noise which might occur on immersion, however, was adequately masked by the loud "whoosh" of the animal's blowing.

The minimum intertrial interval was 2 minutes. During this period, the glass was shifted according to a randomized schedule. The movement of the glass was accomplished in two steps or stages. It was first pushed to the center of the apparatus. After a short delay, it was then either returned to its original position or moved the rest of the way in the same direction so as to close the alternate opening. The noise made by this adjustment was consequently a two-stage affair, and it occurred regularly whether the glass remained in the same location or was changed to the opposite aperture.

The place or position from which Albert started forward in approaching the apparatus was obviously determined on any trial by the porpoise itself. The starting point was consequently not fixed or uniform. As in the size-discrimination study described in chapter 8, estimates of the starting distance from the goal were recorded by E_1 as a part of the data for each trial.

PRELIMINARY TRAINING

A great deal of preliminary training was necessary in this situation in order to familiarize the animal with the procedure, and particularly to overcome its wariness or timidity in the presence of the strange underwater framework. This adaptive training was conducted with the glass removed from the apparatus. At first, the porpoise remained away from the dock and was induced to approach it only by food-fish thrown into the water at closer and closer distances. Finally, a fish could be held by the hand under the water on the porpoise's side of the apparatus. The arm of the feeder at first projected a foot or

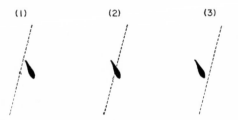

Fig. 17.—Preliminary training was necessary in order to get the animal to insert its mouth through the aperture of the metal frame. Fish were first held in front of the frame as in (*1*), and on successive trials were gradually moved backward through the frame, as in (2) and (3). The glass was removed from the apparatus for these habituating trials.

more in front of the screen. Successive rewards were then moved slowly backward into one or the other of the apertures, until the animal would take the fish from behind the plane of the plywood screen. More than six weeks were required to attain this result.

During this habituation period, a straight piece of No. 9 baling wire ($\frac{5}{16}$ inch in diameter) was mounted parallel to the screen above the water line on the porpoise's side. The wire was used as a kind of sighting device to tell when the subject had approached to within 12 inches of the screen. Time scores to the "foot" position were treated in the results. The mere presence of this wire in the air well above the water, however, at first produced fear reactions, since the porpoise now had to swim *under* something before placing its mouth *inside* the rigid rectangular frame. Indeed, it appeared as if the developing of the necessary adaptation required for the conduct of the formalized experiment constituted a considerable part of the learning so far as the animal itself was concerned.

Pre-training and regular experimental sessions were preceded by food-deprivation periods of 23 hours.

THE MODIFICATION OF BEHAVIOR

The main body of the research—encompassing a period of four additional weeks—included 202 trials divided into 10 experimental sessions. The trials per session and the estimated starting positions per session are given in Table 8.

That learning continued throughout the regular experimental trials is evident from Figure 18, which shows the reduction in the response times per session. The times plotted in this graph were measured from the start of a trial (the insertion of the fishes) to the instant the animal contacted the positive fish. The number of time scores determining each point can be found by reference to Table 8. Since no errors (approaches to the glass) took place throughout the entire experiment, the response times recorded are all for correct trials only. Had the

TABLE 8

APPROACH DISTANCE PER SESSION

Session No.	Trials Per Session	Average Approach Distance in Feet (Estimate)
1	13	5.5
2	18	6.3
3	12	5.9
4	20	5.5
5	20	6.0
6	26	6.6
7	25	6.7
8 *	24	4.3
9 *	24	4.3
10	20	4.5
Total	202	...
Average or weighted average	20.2	5.7

* Night sessions.

visual process been used in making the discriminations, some errors would certainly have occurred.

Further data on the modification of behavior are presented in Figure 19, which gives the average swimming speed in feet per second as the sessions progressd. These results were obtained by dividing the estimated distance of approach (Table 8) by the average time per trial. Swimming speeds computed both to the goal position and to the "foot" position (12 inches in front of the screen) are shown in Figure 19. The difference between these two gives a relative measure of the time spent in the last 12 inches of forward motion.

It will be noted that both speeds tended to become faster with practice, suggesting the development of "confidence" or something like it—although the increase was greater over the first part of the approach distance (start-to-foot) than for the approach distance as a whole (start-to-goal). The speed of swimming in the 12 inches nearest the goal actually slowed down in the later sessions, as indicated by the divergence of the curves.

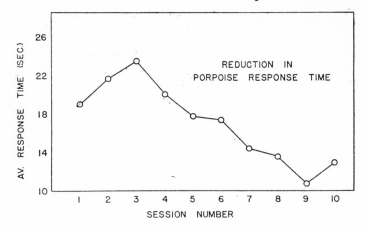

Fig. 18.—The learning or adaptation in the experimental situation is indicated by the gradual reduction in porpoise response times.

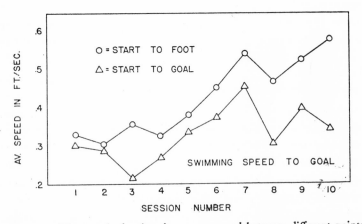

Fig. 19.—The speed of swimming as measured between different points is shown in this figure. The difference between the two curves indicates the amount of time which was spent in the last foot of forward motion.

This means that more time was spent in the 12 inches of space nearest the apparatus. Such a finding is again suggestive of the probable reduction of fear or timidity in what amounted to an approach-avoidance situation.

A surprising and unexpected result in the later trials was the appearance of a new and original porpoise technique for the performance of the task. The animal developed the habit of taking a position in front of the open window *before* the target fish were inserted in the water. Having eaten the available fish from the preceding trial, Albert would then move in front of the unobstructed aperture and wait out the remainder of the intertrial interval—emitting frequent "searching" sound bursts during the waiting period. This seemed to indicate not only that the porpoise was "ready and willing" but that it knew precisely where to go before it had been given any reason for moving. An association had obviously been made between the echoes from the opened window and the forthcoming pattern of echoes to be returned from the positive fish. Immediately after the immersion of the two fishes—when echoes were reflected back from the positive target—the sound signals sent out by the animal became almost continuous, and it swam toward the target with oscillating head movements (see chap. 7).

SONAR RESPONSES AT NIGHT

On two separate occasions, namely, sessions 8 and 9, trials were conducted in near-total darkness at night. The time and response data were relayed by sound-powered telephone to an additional experimenter, (E4), who was located in a blacked-out laboratory building close to the pool. An examination of Table 8 and of Figures 18 and 19 will show that no striking variations occurred in the behavior of the experimental subject under these limiting conditions. There was no significant change in the latency of response, and the accuracy of discrimination remained at 100 per cent. The nighttime control sessions furnish additional evidence that the visual modality was unimportant—if not entirely ignored—in the process of locating the bait.

The only possible effect of the reduction in illumination during the night sessions is indicated in Table 8 by the slightly shorter distances of approach. These distances were estimates made by the experimenter, however, and at night he had to make them with scotopic instead of with photopic vision. There is a real question, therefore, whether the reduction as recorded may not be due to a constant error of human observation rather than to the approaching behavior of the porpoise.

The conclusion is inescapable that the animal discriminated between the visually identical food-fish by means of its own sonar pulses. So far as light rays are concerned, the two stimuli were identical. But the reflection of sound from a large sheet of glass would be utterly different from its reflection from an empty hole containing a small fish. What the porpoise actually distinguished was a big reflecting surface from a very much smaller one—or, in effect, an open window from a closed one. Such a distinction should be vastly easier by echo-ranging than the discrimination between two fishes which was examined in chapter 8.

THE SENSE OF TASTE

The senses to be dealt with in an analysis of this sort are the so-called distance of non-contact senses—that is, the senses which permit the detection of objects from a distance. In this special category belong sight, or vision; hearing; taste; smell; and, possibly, thermal radiation or convection. The visual modality by now should be effectively eliminated as a possible error in porpoise echo-ranging—to the satisfaction of everyone, we hope.

The question of thermal radiation or the convection of thermal currents seems quite fantastic, since none of our targets was either heated or cooled. The food-fish, after defrosting, were kept in pails of sea water from which they were removed individually as they were used. Moreover, infrared vibrations (or heat rays) are not transmitted well in water. The possibility of thermal stimulation can therefore be dropped from serious consideration.

Smell is ruled out, as we have seen on previous occasions, because of the complete absence of the olfactory receptor in the porpoise. The assumption that a porpoise, like a dog, can "smell its way to a fish" is consequently without foundation. There remains, however, the sense of taste, which must now be considered in some detail.

Certainly, the bottlenose dolphin possesses a gustatory sense, and probably a very good one at that. Since chemical taste particles can be given off in the water by food-fish immersed as targets, some of these particles may reach the taste buds of an animal swimming nearby. As a matter of fact, we have already found it expedient to consider taste an important reinforcer in the size-discrimination situation discussed in chapter 8. An extreme position at this point—although a theoretically defensible one—is that a porpoise may need neither vision, hearing, nor smell to find a food-object. For now comes the possibility that it may be able to "taste its way" to a fish. Instead of following its nose, it may simply "follow its taste buds." Obviously, something must be done about this new, and somewhat surprising, loophole.

THE NET EXPERIMENT

What we have to demonstrate is the accuracy of the echo-ranging process without the possibility of any taste substances serving as uncontrolled cues in the solution of the problem. We must not only eliminate vision, but we must eliminate all gustatory stimuli as well. Since we shall now be unable to reward our animals with food, an experiment of this sort would have to make use of the avoidance, rather than the approaching, principle.

The equipment for such a study is diagramed in Figure 20.

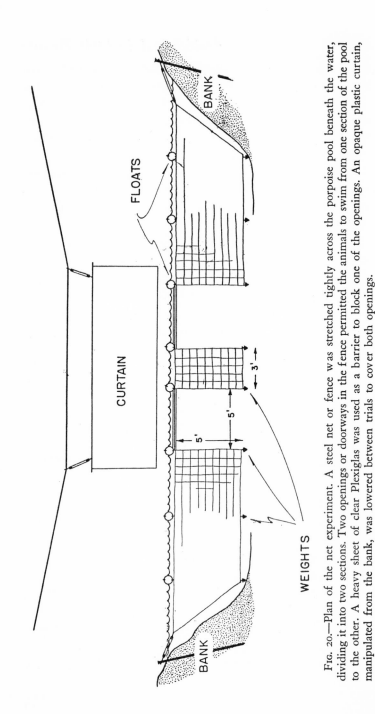

Fig. 20.—Plan of the net experiment. A steel net or fence was stretched tightly across the porpoise pool beneath the water, dividing it into two sections. Two openings or doorways in the fence permitted the animals to swim from one section of the pool to the other. A heavy sheet of clear Plexiglas was used as a barrier to block one of the openings. An opaque plastic curtain, manipulated from the bank, was lowered between trials to cover both openings.

It requires the evasion of an invisible barrier of clear plastic. The subjects of the experiment were two bottlenose dolphins. Albert, as usual, acted as one of them; the other was Betty, a mature female. The results for both of these individuals are combined in the discussion which follows. For convenience, we shall call this experiment "the net experiment."

A submerged net of wire fencing 5 feet in height was stretched tightly across the width of the pool at the center. It formed a fixed partition dividing the water area into two approximately equal parts. The wire in the fencing was ⅛ inch in diameter and was woven into squares 5 inches to the side. The net was supported by floats at the surface and was weighted at the bottom. Two openings 5 feet wide, located near the middle of the partition, were the only passages or doorways from one half of the pool to the other. A large curtain of black war-surplus plastic was suspended from a heavy cable that was stretched across the pool. The curtain could be raised or lowered to block or cover both openings.

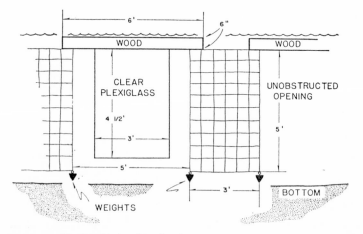

FIG. 21.—The barrier in place for the net experiment whose over-all plan is shown schematically in Figure 20. The door was moved laterally by tackle operated from the bank when the black opaque curtain was submerged and covered both openings.

One of the openings could also be closed by a rigid sheet of clear Plexiglas, as shown schematically in Figure 21. Tackle from the shore permitted the Plexiglas to be moved laterally to block either hole. With the black curtain raised, the porpoises were therefore confronted with a choice situation requiring them to distinguish between the two doorways in the wire fencing, one of which was blocked by a solid but invisible barrier.

MOTIVATION BY AVOIDANCE

Two other nets—which might be called "motivating nets" —were placed at the ends of the pool, one at each end, parallel to the net which divided the pool. These motivating nets were movable and were used to induce the animals to pass from one side of the partition to the other. It should be clearly emphasized that the use of the motivating nets was not a matter of "pushing" the porpoises through an opening by physical contact. As the motivating net slowly advanced, they were simply confined in a smaller and smaller space. Since porpoises tend to avoid contact and will shy away from any strange or unusual object, they would avoid the motivating net behind them by escaping into the open area of the opposite side of the pool. This constituted the completion of a trial.

The black curtain was then lowered and the original motivating net floated back to its starting position. On the next trial, the second motivating net, now behind the animals, was used to make them return to the original half of the pool. The subjects were gradually familiarized with the apparatus and conditions in several preliminary sessions with the Plexiglas removed and with both apertures free and unoccupied.

During the regular experimental trials, the Plexiglas door was adjusted in position only when the black curtain was submerged and completely covered both openings. As in the case of the glass-barrier experiment just described, the lateral movement of the Plexiglas from one side to the other was performed in two stages. The Plexiglas was placed in the center position between the two doorways, and it was then given a final adjustment so as to fill one of the openings. In this way, the apparatus noise was a two-stage affair and was always the same, even though the barrier was moved away from an aperture and returned to its original position. The right-left sequence of the open doorway was randomly determined on successive trials.

The timing of a trial began when the curtain was raised and the choice apparatus exposed to the animals. The timing ended when the animals came up to blow or exhale on the opposite side of the net. The time lag or latency score for any given trial was the interval elapsing between these two events. Since the porpoises could be readily identified by observers, time scores were recorded separately for each.

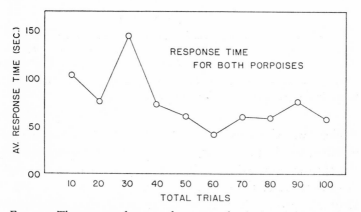

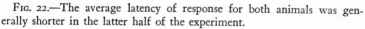

Fig. 22.—The average latency of response for both animals was generally shorter in the latter half of the experiment.

THE LATENCY OF RESPONSE

The quantitative data for the experiment were obtained from 50 trials for each porpoise, or a total of 100 trials for both. Relevant information about the animals and their preferences were brought to light when the latencies or time scores were plotted against trials. The results on this matter are summarized in Figures 22, 23, and 24. The latency measurements for both porpoises combined are shown in Figure 22. Some degree of learning or adaptation to the situation is evident from this graph, as indicated by the lower average values in the later trials compared with those of the earlier trials.

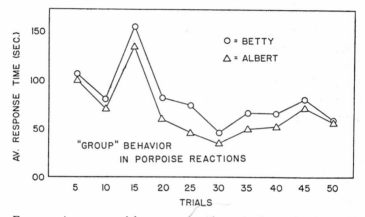

Fɪɢ. 23.—A strong social or group tendency is shown by the similar trends in the response times of the two animals.

There was also a strong tendency for the animals to remain together, and it was not often that one of them passed through the open aperture without the other following soon afterward. A comparison of the time data for the two animals separately (Fig. 23) gives a clear picture of this grouping or social attraction. Albert was almost always the leader in going through the passageway, and Betty, who was more resistant to the situation, was consequently slower. This pattern of response might have been predicted for the older porpoise from what was already known about her general behavior.

An unsuspected difference in their willingness to go through the net seemed to depend on the direction of swimming. They swam from north to south more readily than they went from south to north. It was more difficult, in terms of the length of

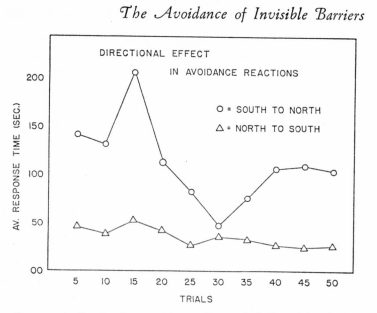

Fig. 24.—A directional or position preference is indicated by the time scores in these curves.

the response time, for the porpoises to proceed in a northerly direction than it was for them to proceed in a southerly direction. In other words, they possessed a strong preference for remaining in, and for returning to, the south half of the pool. Quantitative evidence is given in Figure 24.

This preference is not so difficult to understand when it is considered that they were regularly fed from the dock at the south end and seldom from other positions. Both the size-discrimination experiment and the glass-barrier experiment—each of which made use of positive reinforcement—were conducted in the south half. The surprising thing is that these earlier experiences should have built up so strong an association to return to "home base." This was particularly unusual, in view of the fact that both animals swam freely throughout the entire enclosure and—so far as we were able to determine—remained near the south end only at times of feeding or experimentation.

LOCATION WITHOUT GUSTATION

Within the total of 100 trials for both porpoises, there were two erroneous responses. In other words, two collisions occurred during the total of 100 passages through the net. The accuracy of performance was consequently 98 per cent. When a collision took place, it was at once detected from the bank by a shaking of the net and an angular displacement of the Plexiglas itself.

This efficiency value of 98 per cent was obtained in an experiment in which there could be no question about the participation of the sense of taste. Since the Plexiglas sheet was clear and colorless, it formed an invisible barrier like that employed in the glass-barrier experiment. Other possible sensory avenues, such as olfaction and the temperature sense, were non-existent as potential indicators of the barrier. We are left again with the acoustic modality as the only possible sensory avenue for distinguishing the blocked from the open passageway.

It should be noted, however, that the porpoises not only chose the free instead of the occupied doorway. They also distinguished the 5-inch squares of the fencing itself from a space where there was no wire at all. In view of the turbidity of the water, these gray ⅛-inch strands of steel must have been difficult, if not impossible, to detect by means of the eye.

Chapter 10

A Porpoise
Obstacle Course

Occasionally crabs got into the porpoise pool. Even though a brass grill covered the intake pipes through which sea water flowed, these crustaceans seemed to be able to squeeze through the grill when the tide was high. Since the noises made by the crabs interfered with underwater listening for porpoise sounds, we began introducing a baited crabtrap into the pool at night. By means of the horizontal rigging above the water, we could pull the trap out over the surface and then lower it to the bottom. When this had been done, a quarter-inch manilla rope hung loosely from the pulley on the cable, 10 feet or more above the water, to the crabtrap below. The total length of the rope, from the pulley to the bottom, was 17 or 18 feet. We wondered if this rope would interfere with the navigation of the porpoises —particularly at night.

If the massive body of a moving porpoise were to strike the rope, it would be likely to slide the trap somewhat along the bottom. The top end of the rope was fixed in position by the overhead pulley. The result would be that the rope would no longer hang vertically. We watched diligently for a rope hanging at an angle, but always with completely negative results.

At other times, when it was no longer necessary to keep the crabtrap in the water, we put a light concrete weight (about 2 pounds) on the bottom in the same manner. The tackle was adjusted carefully so that there was just enough slack to permit a lateral movement of the weight along the bottom. An arrangement of this sort remained in the water in some cases for weeks at a time. The rope became slimy and overgrown with green moss. Yet there was never the slightest indication that it had been touched or interfered with in any way. Observations such as this led to the construction of a kind of submerged obstacle course through which the animals were forced to swim.

METALLIC POLES WHICH RING

The obstacles chosen were to be vertical metal poles or rods. These we planned to suspend by one end from the horizontal network of wires and cables. Rigging operated from the bank would enable us to lower these obstructions into the water or to raise them up out of it as desired. A requirement of the method, however, was that we have some way of telling without fail whenever a collision might occur. This information had to be recorded at all times—even when a porpoise was swimming completely submerged near the bottom or in darkness at night.

The problem was finally solved by borrowing from the method used by the animals themselves. That is, we resorted to an auditory, rather than a visual or mechanical, means to register the collisions. To accomplish such a result, it was necessary to construct poles which would give off a noise on contact. These obstacles were made of 28-gauge galvanized sheet iron. They were 52 inches long, with a metal ring at the top end. They therefore subtended most of the vertical distance from

the surface to the bottom. In cross-section, they were triangular
—2 inches to the side. A diagram of one such pole is shown as
item (1) in Figure 9.

Since the obstacles were suspended by lines from above, they
hung freely in the water. Being made of light metal, they were
extremely sensitive to contact stimuli and would give off a
metallic ringing sound if struck, touched, or rubbed lightly—
either in air or in water. As a consequence, a collision by a porpoise with any of these metal obstructions, even though invisible
from the air, was picked up by the hydrophone and recorded
acoustically on magnetic tape. The sounds made by the poles
were so different in both pitch and timbre from the beaming
signals of the animals that there was no possibility of confusing
the two. Data were obtained in this way not only on the echo-
ranging performance in the field of submerged obstacles but
also on the number of collisions which occurred (W. Kellogg,
1959*a*).

Nets stretched across each end of the pool were moved
slightly toward the center to enclose both porpoises within a
square approximately 55 feet to the side. Thirty-six of the metal
obstructions, which completely bracketed the swimming area,
were then simultaneously lowered into the water. Each obstruction was supported from above by a ⅛-inch cotton cord. The
distance between adjacent poles was 8 feet—a distance equivalent to about one porpoise length.

The spatial arrangements for deploying these obstructions
were the "regular" or standard pattern, and the "staggered" pattern. In both of these arrangements, there were six rows of six
poles each. A crew of six assistants was required to manipulate
the somewhat complex rigging—one person handling each row
of obstructions. Two kinds of tackle operated the poles. These
permitted us to place the poles in the desired position above
the water and to raise or lower them vertically. The patterns
regularly employed are diagrammed in Figure 25.

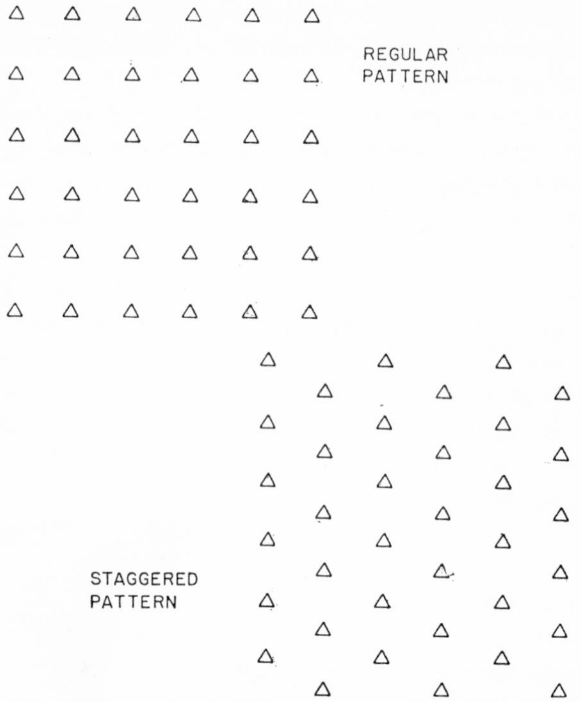

Fig. 25.—Different patterns of metallic obstructions which were lowered into the water in the enclosed area of the obstacle course. The rows and columns in these patterns were 8 feet apart.

SWIMMING BETWEEN THE OBSTRUCTIONS

The test sessions consisted of 20-minute (or longer) periods of swimming through this field of submerged objects. Six sessions of this sort were conducted at irregular intervals over a period of about nine months. During the months when the observations were made, the absolute threshold of visibility, as measured by the Secchi disc, averaged 24.1 inches, with a standard deviation of 10.1 inches.

Contrary to expectations, the animals were found to swim *faster* through the obstructions than they did without them.

146

The poles clearly increased rather than decreased the rate of locomotion. The instant the obstacles were immersed, both porpoises would noticeably accelerate their swimming speed. The direction of swimming was both up and down between the rows and also diagonally at 45 degrees. Generally speaking they remained together, although occasionally this was not the case. If separated, they appeared to seek each other, and when contact had been re-established, they stayed together as a pair.

They also came up for air less frequently and sometimes swam for considerable periods submerged. Had they surfaced more often than usual one might suppose that they were deliberately looking at the ⅛-inch cotton cords which supported the obstacles. It is possible they could locate the obstructions in this way. But such an interpretation will not hold, since the frequency of surfacing was less than usual and occurred only after many poles had been passed and often after new alleys had been entered.

As for collisions, there were four in the first 20-minute session, three in the second, and none in all subsequent tests. It looked as though those collisions which did occur were caused by the protruding tail flukes after the trunk or torso of the animal had actually passed an obstruction. It was no doubt difficult to turn so long a body from one lane into another in such a confining space. The rapid elimination of errors implies that the porpoises *learned* to navigate efficiently within this field of obstacles.

Several possible hypotheses concerning the increase in swimming speed in the obstacle situation may be suggested.

1. The speed-up may have been a fear reaction, like that produced when strange sounds are transmitted into the water. The fact that the animals tended to swim together supports this notion.

2. By moving more rapidly, they may have been better able to locate the posts, since the echoes from a train of signals would thereby change more rapidly. Hence, the process of navigation may have been more precise with a faster rate of movement.

147

3. They may actually have been *playing* in the obstacle course. Their increased activity and continuous swimming up and down the lanes could indicate a kind of playful game-of-tag attitude, rather than a fear response. Although an interpretation of this sort is somewhat unlikely, it fits in with what is known about the porpoise personality. We should consider it, perhaps, as no more than a possibility.

BEAMING TO LOCATE OBSTACLES

The beaming of the sonar signals was continuous in the obstacle course, but surprisingly, it was of *lower* intensity than usual. One assumes that the signals were reduced in loudness to minimize the echoes from more distant poles, which could only have been confusing in such a situation. The large number of obstructions would produce so many different echoes that loud pinging would be useless, or at least more difficult to interpret. The situation might be compared to placing a person in a "hall of mirrors," where he would be disconcerted by seeing so many images of himself. For this reason, the animals may have tuned down their sputtering to a low volume so that the echoes from distant poles would be weaker. The intensity increased momentarily, however, immediately after the submergence of the obstructions. It also increased after the poles had been removed from the water, as if the porpoises were searching for objects which had now disappeared.

Another explanation for the increased intensity of the clicking after the poles had been pulled up was the fact that the water dripping from them made interfering splashing sounds on the surface of the pool. Previous tests had shown that the noise of splashing in the water will initiate sonar signals (chap. 7). To test this question, we carefully adjusted one row of six poles so that the bottom end of each was exactly at the same level. We then observed the beaming reactions (*a*) when the poles were entirely submerged, (*b*) when they were completely above the water and dripping, and (*c*) when all but the bottom inch or so was above the surface. The last arrangement made the poles possible hazards for collision only at the top of the water. Yet it eliminated the sounds of dripping, since the surplus water now flowed silently down the metal surfaces into the pool. Under these circumstances, the pinging signals of the animals did not increase in loudness. The conclusion seems reasonable that the noise of the dripping was the primary stimulus for augmenting their intensity.

When food-fish were thrown into the water with the obstacles still in place, the loudness of the sonar signals also increased. So far as we could tell, it changed to about the intensity level which the animals usually employed when locating or approaching such fishes. However, the tendency to chase after food-fish which were thrown some distance away was obviously hindered by the presence of nearby obstructions. The customary race for the fish did not take place. As a consequence, the porpoises lost many of the fish which were thrown and took only those which landed close by.

JAMMING THE SOUND SIGNALS

To study the effect of interference on the echo-ranging process, sounds were transmitted into the water by the 1K transducer and were broadcast to the animals as they were swimming through the obstructions. In theory, the most disturbing or distracting noises for such a purpose would be the sound pulses emitted by the animals themselves. We therefore took tape recordings of their own sonar signals from an earlier session and broadcast these back to them at a subsequent session. But no collisions occurred, and there were no observable disturbing effects on the swimming or avoidance behavior. The inference is clear that the porpoises distinguished without difficulty between the genuine and the recorded signals. This conclusion is supported by the findings of Griffin and Grinnell (1958) that the echolocation of bats is almost wholly unaffected by jamming or interfering noises.

AVOIDANCE AT NIGHT

A final test with the sheet-metal poles was conducted in nearly complete darkness at night. The sky was mostly cloudy and there was no moon. The closest artificial illumination of any kind was over 5 air-miles away. The amount of ambient light which penetrated the turbid water in which the animals were swimming must, under these conditions, have been very small indeed.

Despite these limiting factors, there was again no decrement in the efficiency of their avoidance behavior. The periods of submersion (detected by sounds of blowing or breathing) were no different in length from those which occurred in the obstacle field during the daytime. The beaming or sonar signals were the same. There were no collisions of any kind. It seems obvious that they could only have avoided the metal obstructions which surrounded them by reacting to echoes from their own beaming signals.

Chapter 11

Conclusion

The object of the series of investigations we have just examined has been to demonstrate the process of sonar or echo-ranging in the bottlenose dolphin, *Tursiops truncatus*. We wanted to find out if a dolphin or porpoise could locate food objects, like fishes, by bouncing echoes off the fishes' bodies. We wanted to discover whether it could avoid submerged obstructions by using its ears alone. We wanted to learn if it could navigate at night or in turbid water without employing vision, touch, or any of the chemical senses. To do this under controlled conditions, we had to eliminate all of the other sensory avenues which these animals might conceivably make use of in such situations. The research program as a whole has extended over some nine years and has included both wild or free-swimming, as well as captive, porpoises.

During the course of these studies, we have been privileged to become acquainted with one of the most fascinating of living creatures—an intelligent and fun-loving animal which has too long escaped scientific attention. Its playfulness and friendliness with man are no less than phenomenal. Its intelligence may rank it even higher than the great apes. The ancients knew the dolphin well and wrote about it frequently, but it would seem that modern man is only just now rediscovering this remarkable animal.

The experiments described in these pages have required us to venture briefly into such divergent fields as oceanography, underwater acoustics, biophysics, physiology, and animal behavior. They also have a bearing on national defense, as a means of improving Navy sonar or echo-ranging. Sonar in the ocean is one of the most important means of navigation below the surface. It takes the place of both vision and radar for a submarine, since neither of these can be used successfully in water. Because the echo-ranging of the porpoise is superior in many respects to the best that man has yet been able to develop, whatever can be learned about it is beneficial.

Our study of porpoise sonar has been divided into three main steps or stages. First, we have analyzed the sound pulses which these animals emit for the purpose of echo-ranging. We sought to determine whether any of their water-borne noises possess the necessary temporal and acoustic characteristics for proper use as sonar signals. Second, we turned to the receiving side to find out if the echoes from porpoise sound pulses could be adequately decoded and analyzed. Lastly, we studied the porpoise in action by examining its ability to use its own sound signals in navigation and in orientation. This last stage has taken up the greater portion of the book.

THE PORPOISE SONAR SYSTEM

The underwater sounds which porpoises produce most often are successive series of rapidly repeated clicks or pings. These noises have been analyzed acoustically by several methods and in several places. They were found to contain a wide band of both sonic and ultrasonic frequencies extending as high as

170,000 cycles per second. Echoes from such clicks have been measured and photographed.

The ear and brain of the animal have been shown to be highly advanced in development. They possess important adaptations for the perception and analysis of underwater sounds. The acoustic receptor is able to compensate for changes in external pressure due to water depth. Porpoises have a much greater range of hearing than human beings and, consequently, respond to many vibrations in the field of ultrasound. The unusual sonar pulses which they send out, and the excellent receptor which they possess, constitute an acute transmitting-receiving mechanism. The brain, moreover, adapted as it is to the sense of hearing, appears to be well equipped to act as a decoder and computer for the neural impulses reaching it.

To investigate the actual working of such a system, we placed captive animals in various experimental situations in a "porpoise laboratory" built for this specific purpose. Much of the apparatus was submerged, and some of it had to be constructed under water. The possibility of the animals' seeing any of the test targets which were used was eliminated by the turbidity of the water. The degree of light penetration into the water of the pool was continually checked.

EXPERIMENTS IN DARKNESS

Another way of eliminating vision which proved effective was to conduct tests during the night, when it was so dark "you couldn't see your hand before your face." Still a third method was to immerse invisible obstructions, like sheets of plate glass and transparent Plexiglas, and to see whether the animals could avoid colliding with them.

We could tell approximately where the porpoises were at night by listening to the sounds of their blowing or exhaling. Some of the submerged obstacles which were used made a metallic noise when struck under water. With these, any collision became *audible* and could be recorded by means of a hydrophone and a tape recorder. In other experiments, we knew when a target had been hit or a food-fish located by the tug or pull which resulted when a porpoise touched it. The nighttime data were relayed by portable telephone to an assistant located in a nearby building which was thoroughly blacked out for the occasion.

SOUND SIGNALS FOLLOW SPLASHES

During intensive work with two experimental subjects, many interesting discoveries came to light. We found, for one thing, that the noise of a splash upon the surface of the water inevitably triggered a series of porpoise sound pulses. The animals appeared to be "looking with their ears" to find out if some foreign object had entered the water. If a splash was made alone, without the immersion of a target, the sputtering signals stopped after a few seconds. When a splash was followed by the presence of some new object in the water, exploratory sound signals continued—presumably until the size and distance of the object had been determined.

Targets placed in the water *without* a splash were perceived in the pool by short bursts or trains of sound signals which occurred spontaneously every 20 seconds or so. We can compare these exploratory pulses only to glancing or peering with the eye. An "auditory glance" which revealed a target would be followed by further trains of investigatory noises. An auditory glance when no target was present ended almost immediately.

Under favorable circumstances, the porpoises could apparently detect an object as small as a single BB shot, $\frac{11}{64}$ of an inch in diameter, by the echo-ranging process.

DISTINGUISHING BETWEEN FISHES

We learned also that porpoises are able to differentiate between food-fish of different sizes by listening to the echoes reflected from the fishes' bodies. This came to light in a discrimination experiment. In the tests which were made, the two fish to be distinguished not only had different reflecting areas, but they were also of different species. One of the fishes was distasteful or unpalatable to the porpoise, and it would reject this variety of fish even after it had one in its mouth. The other or "positive" food-fish was a species which was much sought after.

The distasteful or negative food-fish used in the experiment were chosen so as to be about twice the size of the preferred or positive fish. On any given trial, a positive (small) and a negative (large) fish were simultaneously lowered into the water from behind a visual screen. The positions of the two fishes were randomly alternated. After training, a porpoise was able to approach the smaller fish and ignore the larger one by means of the different echo patterns returning from each fish.

AVOIDING INVISIBLE SURFACES

In another situation, a pair of desirable or preferred food-fish were used as rewards. Each fish was now identical in size and visual appearance; yet the arrangement was such that one of the paired fishes was always offered behind an invisible sheet of plate glass. The remaining fish was readily available and could be taken and eaten by the animal. The glass was sometimes in front of the right-hand fish and sometimes in front of the left-hand fish. If a porpoise relied on vision in such a situation, it would certainly make some approaches to the glass. Yet, because a sheet of glass "sounds different" from a small fish, no mistakes at all occurred in more than 200 trials.

Still a different sort of experiment consisted in having the animals pass through an opening or doorway cut out of a submerged steel fence. There were actually two openings in the fence, but one of them was always blocked by a heavy sheet of transparent Plexiglas. The invisible barrier was randomly adjusted so that it blocked now one doorway, now the other. The porpoises were 98 per cent correct in their solution of this problem.

AN OBSTACLE COURSE FOR PORPOISES

Could we devise an obstacle course for them to swim through? We tried it according to the following plan. Thirty-six sheet-metal poles were suspended over an enclosed area. These could be simultaneosly lowered into the water by assistants who operated tackle from the shore. Only a limited space was allowed for movement between these submerged obstructions. Each pole gave off a bell-like ring when touched or struck, so that collisions were automatically registered on sound-recording tape even though they could not be seen.

A few collisions occurred at first, but as soon as the performers got used to making the short and difficult turns required in this situation, the errors ceased. Even at night, there were no further collisions.

JAMMING SOUNDS ARE INEFFECTIVE

Finally, we endeavored to disturb or jam the echo-ranging signals by making extraneous interfering noises within the pool. The best or most effective interference, we argued, would be reproductions of the porpoises' own sound pulses which had been recorded as they swam among the obstacles at an earlier session. So we played back to them, through an underwater projector, high-fidelity recordings of their own noises, made when they had previously navigated through the obstructions. But no collisions occurred. It seemed obvious that they were able without difficulty to sort out the genuine echoes from the man-made copies which were artificially broadcast.

The question of just how a porpoise makes these sharp staccato sound pulses does not yet seem to be answered to everyone's satisfaction. The same may be said of the birdlike whistle which occurs less frequently. Strictly speaking, a porpoise has no vocal cords. Its "voice"—not being "vocal"—is therefore not a voice. To be exact, one should refer to porpoise sound production as "phonation" rather than "vocalization."

THE COMPLEXITY OF THE PROCESS

Let us emphasize that porpoise sonar is quite a different matter from carrying on a conversation. When we talk, the sound travels fairly directly to the ear of the listener, and the direct sound intensity is much greater than the echoes. In fact, echoes are generally so weak that when they become noticeable in our everyday lives, it is cause for comment. In the sonar method, on the other hand, the basic sounds considered are the echoes, and the task is to isolate one particular kind of echo from others which may be stronger or of different composition. Having isolated it, the further task is to determine the distance, direction, speed, size, shape, and possibly the texture of the object producing that echo. When one considers the complexity of events involved in the process, the whole problem appears fantastically difficult.

As one example, let us consider a single sonar ping coming from a porpoise. This will reach both surface and bottom, whence it will be returned as surface and bottom reverberation —an indefinite type of rumble. All the objects in the water also contribute to the rumble. Every object within range will produce an echo not only from the direct beam but also from beams reflected from the surface, from the bottom, from surface to bottom, and from bottom to surface. Echoes will return not only via a direct path but also via the various reflected pathways. These subsidiary echoes must be either sorted out and ignored or used in some way for the spatial orientation of the porpoise with reference to the primary object.

The particular characteristics of an echo will depend on the size, shape, distance, and the absorption coefficient of the surface returning the echo. They will also depend on the frequencies contained in the sonar signal. The degree of interpretation and analysis which follows the sensory reception of each echo depends, in turn, on the ability of the computing system (the brain) which deals with these variables. Imagine, for example, the recording of a piano concerto that is being played on a hi-fi set. *Hearing* the recording is not much of a problem. Perceiving it as a concerto, identifying the composer, recognizing the particular work and movement, and even the recording artist, require more and more background information. Obviously, in the problem of perception, the intelligence and previous learning of the observer are of paramount importance.

Echolocation is not just sensing the presence of an echo. It requires the ability to interpret, evaluate, and identify that echo. This complex avenue of auditory perception seems to be quite beyond the capacity of an ordinary man, who makes little use of it in his own surroundings.

References

ALPERS, A. *A book of dolphins.* London: John Murray, 1960

ANDERSON, J. W. The production of ultrasonic sounds by laboratory rats and other animals. *Science* **119:** 808–9. 1954.

BACKHOUSE, K. Locomotion and direction-finding in whales and dolphins. *New Scientist* **7:** 26–28. 1960.

BEALE, T. *The natural history of the sperm whale.* 2d ed. London: J. Van Voorst, 1839.

BEDDARD, F. E. *A book of whales.* London: John Murray, 1900.

BEEBE, W. A round trip to Davy Jones's locker. *Nat. Geog.* **59:** 653–78. 1931.

————. A half mile down. *Nat. Geog.* **66:** 661–704. 1934.

BENHAM, W. B. On the larynx of certain whales. *Proc. Zool. Soc. London* **1:** 287–300. 1901.

BENNETT, F. D. *Narrative of a whaling voyage around the globe, from the year 1833 to 1836.* Vol. II. London: R. Bentley, 1840.

BOSANQUET, F. C. T. *The letters of Caius Plinius Caecilius Secundus.* London: George Bell & Sons, 1909.

159

References

BRAND, A. R., and KELLOGG, P. P. The range of hearing of
canaries. Science 90: 354. 1939.
BRAZIER, M. A. (ed.). The central nervous system and be-
havior. New York: Josiah Macy, Jr., Foundation (Second
Conference), 1959.
BREATHNACH, A. S. The cetacean central nervous system. Biol.
Rev. (Cambridge Phil. Soc.) 35 (2): 187–229. 1960.
CALDWELL, D. K., and FIELDS, H. M. Surf-riding by Atlantic
bottlenose dolphins. J. Mammal. 40: 454–55. 1959.
CARLSON, A. J., and JOHNSON, V. The machinery of the body.
3d ed. Chicago: University of Chicago Press, 1953.
CARSON, R. L. The sea around us. New York: Oxford Uni-
versity Press, 1951.
CHERNISS, H., and HELMBOLD, W. C. Plutarch's Moralia.
Cambridge, Mass.: Harvard University Press, 1957.
CUNNINGHAM, D. J. The spinal nervous system of the porpoise
and dolphin. J. Anat. 11: 209–28. 1877.
DASHIELL, J. F. The role of vision in spatial orientation in the
white rat. J. Comp. Physiol. Psychol. 52: 522–26. 1959.
DICE, L. R., and BARTO, E. Ability of mice of the genus Per-
omyscus to hear ultrasonic sounds. Science 116: 110–11. 1952.
DOBRIN, M. B. Measurements of underwater noise produced
by marine life. Science 105: 19–23. 1947.
———. Recording sounds of undersea life. Trans. New York
Acad. Sci., pp. 91–96. 1948.
DWORKIN, S. Hearing tests in normal operated dogs and cats.
Trans. Amer. Otol. Soc. 24: 143–51. 1934.
ELDER, J. H. The upper limit of hearing in chimpanzees. Amer.
J. Physiol. 112: 109–15. 1935.
ESSAPIAN, F. S. The birth and growth of a porpoise. Nat. Hist.
62 (November): 392–99. 1953.
———. Speed-induced skin folds in the bottle-nosed porpoise,
Tursiops truncatus. Breviora (Mus. Comp. Zool., Harvard)
43: 1–4. 1955.
EWER, R. F. Whales. New Biology 2: 53–73. 1947.

160

EWING, M., and WORZEL, J. L. Long-range sound transmission, in propagation of sound in the ocean. *Geol. Soc. Amer. Mem.,* No. 27. 1948.

FISH, M. P. The character and significance of sound production among fishes of the western North Atlantic. *Bull. Bingham Oceanographic Collection* **14.** 1954*a*.

————. The sonic marine animal problem. *Research Reviews* (U.S. Office of Naval Research), Dec., pp. 180–83. 1954*b*.

FISH, M. P., KELSEY, A. S., and MOWBRAY, W. H. Studies on the production of underwater sound by North Atlantic coastal fishes. *J. Marine Res.* **11:** 180–93. 1952.

FRASER, F. C. Sound emitted by dolphins. *Nature* **160:** 759. 1947.

FRASER, F. C., and PURVES, P. E. Hearing in cetaceans. *Bull. British Museum (Nat. Hist.), Zool.* **2:** 101–14. 1954.

————. Anatomy and function of the cetacean ear. *Proc. Royal Soc.* **152** (B): 62–77. 1960.

FRINGS, H., and FRINGS, M. Duplex nature of reception of simple sounds in the scape moth *Ctenucha virginica*. *Science* **126:** 24. 1957.

GALAMBOS, R. Cochlear potentials from the bat. *Science* **93:** 215. 1941.

GILMORE, R. M. Whales without flukes. *Pacific Naturalist* **1:** 1–9. 1959.

GODLEY, A. D. *Herodotus, with an English transaltion.* Vol. I. New York: Putnam, 1920.

GOULD, J., and MORGAN, C. Hearing in the rat at high frequencies. *Science* **94:** 168. 1941.

GRIFFIN, D. R. Acoustic orientation in the oil bird *Steatornis*. *Proc. Nat. Acad. Sci.* **39:** 884–93. 1953.

————. *Listening in the dark.* New Haven: Yale University Press, 1958.

GRIFFIN, D. R., and GRINNELL, A. D. Ability of bats to discriminate echoes from louder noise. *Science* **128:** 145–46. 1958.

GUNTER, G. Contributions to the natural history of the bottle-nosed dolphin, *Tursiops truncatus* (Montagu), on the Texas coast, with particular reference to food habits. *J. Mammal.* **23:** 267–76. 1942.

GUTENBERG, B. Low-velocity layers in the earth, ocean, and atmosphere. *Science* **131:** 959–65. 1960.

HAAN, F. W. R. Hearing in whales. *Acta Oto-laryngologia,* Suppl. 134. 1957.

———. Some aspects of mammalian hearing under water. *Proc. Royal Soc.* **152** (B) : 54–62. 1960.

HARLOW, H. F. Forward conditioning, backward conditioning and pseudo-conditioning in the goldfish. *J. genet. Psychol.* **55:** 49–58. 1939.

HAYES, W. D. Wave-riding dolphins. *Science* **130:** 1657–58. 1959.

HORTON, J. W. *Fundamentals of sonar.* 2d ed. Annapolis, Md.: U.S. Naval Institute, 1959.

HOWELL, A. B. *Aquatic mammals; their adaptations to life in water.* Springfield, Ill.: Thomas, 1930.

HUBBS, C. L. Dolphin protecting dead young. *J. Mammal.* **34:** 498. 1953.

JAPAN. FISHERIES AGENCY. Propagation characteristics of high frequency ultrasonics in sea water. *Technical Report of Fishing Boat Laboratory* (Tokyo), No. 6, pp. 93–103. March, 1955.

———. Propagation characteristics of high frequency ultrasound in sea water (cont.). *Ibid.,* No. 8, pp. 103–12. March, 1956.

———. Noise of creatures in sea in region of ultrasound. *Ibid.,* No. 12, pp. 99–135. October, 1958.

———. Detection of fish by sonobuoy. *Ibid.,* No. 13, pp. 95–101. October, 1959.

JOHNSON, M. W. Underwater noise and distribution of snapping shrimp with special reference to the Asiatic and Southwest and Pacific areas. PB 40788 (University of California Division of War Research Rept. U146), pp. 1–7. 1944.

JOHNSON, M. W., EVEREST, F. A., and YOUNG, R. W. The role of snapping shrimp (*Cragnon* and *Synalpheus*) in the production of underwater noise in the sea. *Biol. Bull.* 93 (No. 2): 122–38. 1947.

KELLOGG, R. The history of whales. Their adaptation to life in water. *Quart. Rev. Biol.* 3: 174–208. 1928.

———. Whales, giants of the sea. *Nat. Geog.* 77: 35–90. 1940.

KELLOGG, W. N. Bibliography of the noises made by marine organisms. *Amer. Museum Novitates,* No. 1611, pp. 1–5. 1953*a*.

———. Ultrasonic hearing in the porpoise. *J. comp. physiol. Psychol.* 46: 446–50. 1953*b*.

———. Sounds of sea animals (phonograph record). *Folkways Records* (New York). 1955.

———. Echo ranging in the porpoise. *Science* 128: 982–88. 1958*a*.

———. On the psychological study of small whales. *J. Psychol.* 46: 97–100. 1958*b*.

———. Auditory perception of submerged objects by porpoises. *J. acoust. Soc. Amer.* 31: 1–6. 1959*a*.

———. Size-discrimination by reflected sound in a bottlenose dolphin. *J. comp. physiol. Psychol.* 52: 509–14. 1959*b*.

———. Auditory scanning in the dolphin. *Psychol. Record* 10: 25–27. 1960.

KELLOGG, W. N., and KOHLER, R. Responses of the porpoise to ultrasonic frequencies. *Science* 116: 250–52. 1952.

KELLOGG, W. N., KOHLER, R., and MORRIS, H. N. Porpoise sounds as sonar signals. *Science* 117: 239–43. 1953.

KELLOGG, W. N., and SPANOVICK, P. Respiratory changes during the conditioning of fish. *J. comp. physiol. Psychol.* 46: 124–28. 1953.

KRAMER, M. O. The dolphin's secret. *New Scientist* **7**: 1118–20. 1960.

KRITZLER, H. Observations on the pilot whale in captivity *J. Mammal.* **33**: 321–34. 1952.

KRUGER, L. The thalamus of the dolphin (*Tursiops truncatus*) and comparison with other mammals. *J. comp. Neurol.* **111**: 133–94. 1959.

KULLENBERG, B. Sound emitted by dolphins. *Nature* **160**: 648. 1947.

LANGWORTHY, O. R. Central nervous system of the porpoise *Tursiops truncatus. J. Mammal.* **12**: 381–89. 1931a.

——. Factors determining the differentiation of the cerebral cortex in sea-living mammals (the Cetacea). A study of the brain of the porpoise, *Tursiops truncatus. Brain* **54**: 225–36. 1931b.

——. A description of the central nervous system of the porpoise (*Tursiops truncatus*). *J. comp. Neurol.* **54**: 437–99. 1932.

LAWRENCE, B., and SCHEVILL, W. E. The functional anatomy of the delphinid nose. *Bull. Museum comp. Zool.* (Harvard) **114** (No. 4): 103–51. 1956.

LIFE MAGAZINE. A tot-toting dolphin. *Life* **40** (April 23): 105–10. 1956.

LILLY, J. C. Some considerations regarding basic mechanisms of positive and negative types of motivation. *Amer. J. Psychiat.* **115**: 498–504. 1958.

LOYE, D. P., and PROUDFOOT, O. A. Underwater noise due to marine life. *J. acoust. Soc. Amer.* **18**: 446–49, 1946.

MCBRIDE, A. F. Meet mister porpoise. *Nat. Hist.* **45** (January): 16–29. 1940.

MCBRIDE, A. F., and HEBB, D. O. Behavior of the captive bottle-nose dolphin, *Tursiops truncatus. J. comp. physiol. Psychol.* **41**: 111–23. 1948.

MCBRIDE, A. F., and KRITZLER, H. Observations on pregnancy,

parturition, and post-natal behavior in the bottlenose dolphin. *J. Mammal.* **32:** 251–66. 1951.

MOORE, J. C. Distribution of marine mammals in Florida waters. *Amer. Midland Naturalist* **49:** 117–58. 1953.

————. Bottle-nosed dolphins support remains of young. *J. Mammal.* **36:** 466–67. 1955.

MORRIS, H. N., KOHLER, R., and KELLOGG, W. N. Ultrasonic porpoise communications. *Electronics* **26** (No. 8): 208–14. 1953.

MOULTON, J. M. Influencing the calling of sea robins (*Prionotus spp.*) with sound. *Biol. Bull.* **111:** 393–98. 1956.

————. *References dealing with animal acoustics, particularly of marine forms.* Brunswick, Me.: Bowdoin College, Author, 1960.

MOULTON, J. M. and BACKUS, R. H. Annotated references concerning the effects of man-made sounds on the movements of fishes. *Dept. of Sea and Shore Fisheries* (Augusta, Me.) *Circ. No. 117.* 1955.

NATURAL HISTORY. Saved by a porpoise. *Nat. Hist.* **58** (November): 385–86. 1949.

NORMAN, J. R., and FRASER, F. C. *Field book of giant fishes.* New York: Putnam, 1949.

PARRY, SIR WILLIAM EDWARD. *Journal of a voyage for the discovery of the north-west passage from the Atlantic to the Pacific.* London: John Murray, 1821.

PAVLOV, I. P. *Conditioned reflexes.* Oxford: Oxford University Press, 1927.

PICCARD, A. *Earth, sea and sky.* Oxford: Oxford University Press, 1956.

PIERCE, G. W. *The songs of insects.* Cambridge, Mass.: Harvard University Press, 1948.

RACKHAM, H. *Pliny, Natural history, with an English translation.* Vol. III. Cambridge, Mass.: Harvard University Press, 1947.

RILEY, D. A., and ROSENZWEIG, M. R. Echolocation in rats. *J. comp. physiol. Psychol.* **50:** 323–28. 1957.

ROMER, A. S. *Man and the vertebrates.* Chicago: University of Chicago Press, 1957.

SCHEVILL, W. E., and LAWRENCE, B. Underwater listening to the white porpoise (*Delphinapterus leucas*). *Science* **109:** 143–44. 1949.

————. Auditory response of a bottlenosed porpoise, *Tursiops truncatus,* to frequencies above 100 kc. *J. exper. Zool.* **124:** 147–65. 1953*a*.

————. High-frequency auditory response of a bottlenosed dolphin, *Tursiops truncatus* (Montagu). *J. acoust. Soc. Amer* **25:** 1016–17. 1953*b*.

————. *Tursiops* as an experimental subject. *J. Mammal.* **35:** 225–32. 1954.

————. Food-finding by a captive porpoise (*Tursiops truncatus*). *Breviora* (Mus. Comp. Zool., Harvard) **53:** 1–15, 1956.

SCHEVILL, W. E., and MCBRIDE, A. F. Evidence for echolocation by cetaceans. *Deep-sea Res.* **3:** 153–54. 1956.

SCHOLANDER, P. F. Wave-riding of dolphins: how do they do it? *Science* **129:** 1085–87. 1959.

SCHREIBER, O. W. Some sounds from marine life in the Hawaiian area. *J. acoust. Soc. Amer.* **24:** 116. 1952.

SIEBENALER, J. B., and CALDWELL, D. K. Cooperation among adult dolphins. *J. Mammal.* **37:** 126–28. 1956.

SMITH, W., and CHEETHAM, S. *A dictionary of Christian antiquities.* Vol. II. London: John Murray, 1908.

STEBBINS, E. B. *The dolphin in the literature and art of Greece and Rome.* Menasha, Wis.: George Banta, 1929.

TAVOLGA, W. N. Foghorn sounds beneath the sea. *Nat. Hist.* **69** (March): 44–49. 1960.

THOMPSON, W. D. *The works of Aristotle translated into English.* Vol. IV. Oxford: Clarendon Press, 1910.

TOI, P. Opo the gay dolphin. *Te Ao Hou* (Dept. Maori Affairs, New Zealand) **6** (No. 3): 22–24. 1958.

Tomilin, A. G. A contribution to the biology and physiology of *Delphinus delphis* (L). *C. R. (Doklady) Acad. Sci. URSS* **56**: 221–23. 1947*a*.

———. A new interpretation of spouts in cetaceans. *Ibid.* **55**: 81–84. 1947*b*.

Townsend, C. H. Porpoises at sea. *Bull. Zool. Soc. N.Y.* **19**: 1427–28. 1916.

U.S. Fish and Wildlife Service. Attempts to guide small fish with underwater sound. *Special Sci. Rept.: Fisheries* No. 111. Washington, D.C., 1953.

Vincent, F. Études preliminaires de certaines émissions acoustique de *Delphinus delphia* L. en captivité. *Bull. Inst. Océanog.* (Monaco) **57** (No. 1172): 1–23. 1960.

Von Gierke, H. E., *et al.* Physics of vibrations in living tissues. *J. appl. Physiol.* **4**: 886–900. 1952.

Wever, E. G., and Bray, C. W. A new method for the study of hearing in insects. *J. cell. comp. Physiol.* **4**: 79–93. 1933.

———. A comparative study of the electrical response of the ear. *Proc. Amer. Phil. Soc.* **78**: 407–10. 1937.

Wood, F. G., Jr. Porpoise sounds. Underwater sounds made by *Tursiops truncatus* and *Stenella plagiodon* (phonograph record). Marineland Research Lab. 1952.

———. Underwater sound production and concurrent behavior of captive porpoises *Tursiops truncatus* and *Stenella plagiodon*. *Bull. Marine Sci. of the Gulf and Caribbean* **3**: 120–33. 1953.

Woodcock, A. H. The swimming of dolphins. *Nature* **161**: 602. 1948.

Woodcock, A. H., and McBride, A. F. Wave-riding dolphins. *J. exp. Biol.* **28**: 215–17. 1951.

Woodworth, R. S., and Schlossberg, H. *Experimental psychology*. New York: Holt, 1954.

Worthington, L. V., and Schevill, W. E. Underwater sounds heard from sperm whales. *Nature* **180**: 291. 1957.

Yamada, N. Contribution to the anatomy of the organ of hearing of whales. *Whales Res. Inst. Sci. Rept.* **8**: 1–79. 1953.

YAMADA, N., and YOSHIZAKI, F. Oceous labyrinth of cetacea. *Whales Res. Inst. Sci. Rept.* **14:** 291–304. 1959.

YERKES, R. M. The sense of hearing in frogs. *J. comp. neurol. Psychol.* **15:** 279–304. 1905.

ZIPF, G. K. *Human behavior and the principle of least effort.* Cambridge, Mass.: Addison-Wesley Press, 1949.

Index

169